The Family Business

The Family Business

ROBERT MARSDEN

BAAF
ADOPTION
& FOSTERING

Published by
British Association for Adoption & Fostering
(BAAF)
Saffron House
6–10 Kirby Street
London EC1N 8TS
www.baaf.org.uk

Charity registration 275689

British Library Cataloguing in Publication Data
A catalogue record for this book is available from the British
Library

ISBN 978 1 905664 32 0

Project management by Shaila Shah,
Director of Publications, BAAF
Photograph on cover © Ed Marsden
Designed by Andrew Haig & Associates
Typeset by Fravashi Aga
Printed in Great Britain by Athenaeum Press Ltd.
Trade distribution by Turnaround Publisher Services, Unit 3,
Olympia Trading Estate, Coburg Road, London N22 6TZ

BAAF is the leading UK-wide membership organisation for all
those concerned with adoption, fostering and child care issues.

The paper used for the text pages of this book is FSC certified.
FSC (The Forest Stewardship Council) is an international network
to promote responsible management of the world's forests.

Printed on chlorine-free paper.

FSC
Mixed Sources
Product group from well-managed
forests and other controlled sources
Cert no. SGS-COC-2482
www.fsc.org
© 1996 Forest Stewardship Council

Acknowledgements

Thanks to Hedi Argent for her advice, support and encouragement in writing this book. Thanks too to friends and family who have both knowingly and unknowingly given me the time to put this little book together. Special thanks to my wife for tweaking the drafts and for toning down the more libellous passages, and to her and the children for their patience, humour, and willingness to be exposed to the public, even if their names have been changed!

About the author

Robert Marsden was born in Newcastle on Tyne and brought up in Cumbria. He trained as a social worker more years ago than he cares to remember, and has spent most of his life working with children. He has had a number of short works of fiction published by Polygon, Fish Publishing, New Writing Scotland and others.

The Our Story series
This book is part of BAAF's Our Story series, which explores adoption experiences as told by adoptive parents.

Also available in this series: *An Adoption Diary* by Maria James, *Flying Solo* by Julia Wise, *In Black and White* by Nathalie Seymour and *Adoption Undone* by Karen Carr.

The series editor
Hedi Argent is an independent family placement consultant, trainer and freelance writer. She is the author of *Find me a Family* (Souvenir Press, 1984), *Whatever Happened to Adam?* (BAAF, 1998), *Related by Adoption* (BAAF, 2004), *Ten Top Tips for Placing Children in Families* (BAAF, 2006) and *Josh and Jaz have Three Mums* (BAAF, 2007). She is the co-author of *Taking Extra Care* (BAAF, 1997, with Ailee Kerrane), and *Dealing with Disruption* (BAAF, 2006, with Jeffrey Coleman), and the editor of *Keeping the Doors Open* (BAAF, 1988), *See You Soon* (BAAF, 1995) *Staying Connected* (BAAF, 2002), and *Models of Adoption Support* (BAAF, 2003). She has also written five illustrated booklets in the children's series published by BAAF: *What Happens in Court?* (2003, with Mary Lane), *What is Contact?* (2004), *What is a Disability?* (2004), *Life Story Work* (2005, with Shaila Shah) and *Kinship Care* (BAAF, 2007).

For children who wait

Contents

1

Prologue: an introduction to William

Our house reverberates to a mixture of musical genres: when all our children are at home, Ed, now nearly twenty-one, and Robbie, seventeen, can be upstairs on bass and drum-kit respectively, beating out heavy metal, while Kate, nineteen, might be in the front room improvising jazz on her harp. Like many ten-year-olds, William likes listening to the band, McFly. Evie and I like Radio 3 ('Why do you have to listen to this rubbish?' queries William every time). But it's his choice this morning. He tells me the group is named after the hero from the film, *Back to the Future*. I've no idea, but he's usually right about these things.

William and I are sitting in the conservatory eating breakfast. It's a Saturday; free time for all of us. Evie is in the shower; Robbie is still in bed; Ed and Kate are away at university. Spring is early and the grass needs cutting. It's on the list in my head, like lots of other things. There's a robin's nest in the woodpile in the garden. The hen bird stares back at me, eyes like shining blackcurrants, each time I stand on tiptoes to look. I've told William about it.

He wanted to see, but I couldn't lift him up high enough, so he's lost interest. Maybe he'll see the babies when they fledge, if the surrounding cats don't get them first.

'Try not to drool, William,' I say between sips of coffee; I've finished eating my breakfast.

'I can't help it,' he answers, a bit reproachfully.

'I know it's difficult, but try to suck and swallow. And keep your mouth closed when you chew.'

He sucks and swallows for half a second, and then opens his mouth while I introduce a fork, speared with cut-up bacon and fried egg. Not at all appetising, now that it's been sitting on the plate for half an hour or so. Mealtimes are still a slow and laborious business.

'You should really be eating this by yourself, you know, William.'

He's good at ignoring things that he doesn't want to hear. He opens his mouth and some saliva, yellow from the egg, falls to his plate. I hand him a piece of kitchen towel, and he thrusts it towards his mouth, his head twisting about spasmodically, then dabs at his chin a bit randomly.

'William?'

He doesn't answer. He's listening to his music and has a couple of Star Wars figures in his hands. He clashes them together in violent battle. He's memorised all six screenplays from watching the films.

'Tell you what, William.'

He looks up to confirm he's listening.

'You eat five more forks-full yourself and we'll stop.'

'Two.' He's become a crafty haggler.

'Four.'

'Three.'

'Okay.'

He launches a forkful, which I have pre-loaded, into his mouth, and chomps away with his mouth open.

'I'm so sick of being lonely,' goes the McFly lyric. It's trite, and full of teenage self-pity. The music sounds as if it had been composed by computer, but the minor key still strikes at the insides.

'Do you think this is a sad song, Daddy?' He crashes the figures together again. 'Aagh!'

'What do you think?'

'I asked you first.'

'Yes, I think it's quite sad.'

'So do I,' he says, maybe now feeling it's okay to say that.

'I'm singing such a sad song,' continues the singer. William crashes the Star Wars figures together again, but loses his grip on one and it clatters to the floor. He grunts at me and points. I raise my eyebrows. 'Please will you pick it up,' he says. I bend to retrieve the figure and feel a familiar twinge in my back.

'Time for another forkful, William. Try and get it on your fork by yourself, this time.'

I wonder if the words of the song have sunk in. William doesn't have any real friends. Sometimes children come round to play, and occasionally he's invited back, but it's more a case of toleration on their part, than the exchange of love and the sharing of secret worlds that makes childhood friendships so special. I wished he didn't drool. It's got worse in the last year. In the scheme of things it sounds like a minor problem, but it's hardly the way to endear him to other children. We think it probably isn't helped by the medication he takes to counter the tightening of his hamstrings. But who knows for sure? It's a bit frustrating, because he's a bright boy, and we often wonder why he can't control his drooling. It doesn't seem like a hard task to us, for whom sucking and swallowing are instinctive and automatic, but he just can't do it, so that's that. It doesn't stop us from encouraging him to try though; to make him more aware and to trigger some sort of connection between thought and action.

He's got a serene, faraway look as he listens to the music, and it seems like a good time to talk.

'What do you think are the good things about being adopted, William?' I ask in a matter-of-fact sort of way.

He looks at me, and I wipe his chin, yellow from drool and egg.

'I'd like to see what my old family is like now,' he says.

I smile at him. It's always the same: a chain of thoughts that leads back to his birth family.

'Yes, but what about being adopted? What are the good things, do you think?'

'Er, let me think.' He's like a little old man when he's in this sort of mood: like his hero, Yoda, from *Star Wars*. 'If I was with my old family I might have to go to bed at half past seven. And that's too early for a boy my age.'

Bedtime is a source of some dispute with William. Through a mixture of wearing us down and skilful negotiation he's stretched out the time to nine p.m.

'Have a forkful of breakfast, please. Remember our deal.' He lifts the forkful to his mouth; I've given up waiting for him to spear the food himself and have loaded it ready for him again.

'You know that thing when your sugar balance is funny, what do you call it again?' He's off at a tangent. He likes his tangents – always going along some mysterious pathway or other.

'Diabetes?'

'Yes, that's it. It must be like looking at something in a dream or something, do you think?' The forkful goes in at last.

'If someone with diabetes falls into a coma, you mean?' We've got used to working out where he's going with his conversations, but Lord knows where this has all come from.

'Yes,' he says, beginning to chew.

'Yes, I suppose so, a bit, though I don't know for sure. Get your next mouthful ready.'

'I've had three.'

'Have you?' I've lost track. I shove one in anyway; he's too preoccupied to object. 'But can you think of any other good things about being adopted?' He begins to retch. 'Chew, William chew,' I say gently. I pass him his cup of milk and he takes a gulp. The spasm subsides again. 'The good things about being adopted?' I remind him.

'I've got a sister.' He's given Kate a hard time over the years. He's repeating something he's heard: 'Aren't you lucky to have such a lovely sister!'

'Yes, that's one thing.'

'And my mummy loves me and I've got a funny daddy.' He knows what to say to please and how to pull the right strings. He lays his hand on the table. It's a cue; I give it a little squeeze, I draw it up to my lips and plant a kiss on his knuckles.

'Anything else?' I ask.

'I wouldn't have known Ed,' the older brother whom he adores.

There's a pause. 'And Robbie,' I prompt.

'Old big ears!' he says with a grin.

I respond with a frown and let go of his hand. He's going through a phase of calling Robbie silly names. Probably a mark of affection – he did the same to the others when they were younger, but it is wearing a bit thin.

'You know that washing thing in the battery-operated Thomas set?' he asks.

Another tangent and a bit more regression. Thomas the Tank Engine featured large in his early years; he would immerse himself for ages in solitary games with his collection of engines, while the videos played till he knew them by heart. (The Reverend W Awdry has a lot to answer for. And how on earth did Ringo Starr get the job as narrator?) I know the toy he means: a cylindrical foam washing device for the engines.

'Yes,' I reply, having worked it out.

'I'd like to build that again sometime.'

'Okay. We'll have a look for it and put it together sometime,' though I hope he'll forget; it will mean a hunt through boxes of toys and fiddling around with batteries and Phillips-head screwdrivers, which of course will take ages to find among the boxes of jumble in the garden shed. 'So, anything else that's good about being adopted?'

'I'd quite like to know my old family, daddy.'

'Yes, I know.' To us they're really just a story. 'Nothing else that's good about being in this family though?'

'Something good.'

'Yes, what's that?'

He pauses, and I look at him expectantly. 'I don't know,' he says at last. 'What are these square bits dad?' He's picked up a plastic Thomas engine and is pointing to a bit of moulding on the front.

'I'm not sure. It's just the shape of the engine I think. Just the way it's made.'

'How do you make an engine?'

'A real one, do you mean?'

'Yes.' He's turning the toy over in his hands.

'I don't know. You need lots of metal though. You'll have to ask Granddad – he's the engineer.'

'You know the Thomas engine we saw in the railway museum in York?'

'Yes.'

'What was the face made of?'

'Metal or wood I should think.' I have one last go at our other conversation. 'So do you think it was a good thing that we adopted you?'

He drops the engine, and it crashes to the floor. I bend to retrieve it and hand it back.

'Yea. A good thing. Can I go and watch television now?'

'Okay, if you push yourself through to the pink room.' Actually the room we keep the TV in is painted yellow. It used to be a pretty awful shade of pink, before we adopted William, and the name's just stuck.

He lets off his brakes and begins wheeling himself slowly through to the lounge, singing along with McFly till he's out of range.

* * *

William's honorary godfather (the husband of one of his official godmothers) calls him a "right Teuchter". He's got stunning ginger hair that gleams in the sun, and pale skin with a hint of freckles. He sits in front of his mirror applying hair gel (it's a messy business) till he's achieved just the right spiky, wild look. When I took him to school the other day his teacher said, 'Oh dear, William, you must have had a rough night; your hair's all over the place'. I told her, in a lowered voice, about the work that had gone into it, and she muttered kindly to William about being out of touch with today's styles.

William has a cheeky sense of humour and blue eyes that sparkle when he laughs. And he laughs an awful lot: spontaneously and innocently at life's nonsense. He laughs when his granddad dozes in his chair and begins to snore; at the budgie, when it perches on Evie's head; at the increasing number of spoonerisms I seem to come out with as I age.

William has long, delicate fingers.

William sings from the heart when no one is looking, screwing up his face to get the right pitch and sound.

He listens to stories with avid concentration – 'Can I have just one more chapter, pleeease?' – *Treasure Island* is the current work in progress, unabridged and full of ancient nautical terms that I don't really understand myself, but he gets the drift.

William has a vocabulary that surprises everyone, and an astonishing memory, which comes in very useful. 'What's the name of the physio who's coming today William?' Quick as a flash. 'It's Judith.'

He gets engrossed in his own little world of computer

games and make-believe. He plays complicated games with his toy figures, despite very limited dexterity; they plunge about crudely in his hands, but he knows all about their complex missions.

William loves company and yearns for friendships. He is uninhibited with adults – 'What's that man got tattooed on his back, Dad?' He asked loudly in the swimming pool changing room recently. 'Shh William,' I hissed, but there was no need. 'Eh? What's that son? He's the King, son, the King.' And the semi-naked bearer rippled his muscles so that Elvis gyrated on his back for William to see. More questions: 'Why did you do it? Did it hurt? Will it come off?' and so on, till the two had struck up a friendship and William had been given an open invitation to ride free on the man's buses anytime. The man turned out to be a bus driver; we had much of his life story by the time he'd finished spraying his Brut around his armpits.

When William cries, his face folds at the corners, and it feels like the tears of misery might never stop. He tilts towards you, held by the restraining belt of his wheelchair, and you bury his head against your chest, and talk and console him till his distress passes. Your heart goes out to him and you want to make it all better. You'd do anything for your children, wouldn't you?

* * *

But William can have his moments…

The other day Evie told him that it was time to come off the computer: he'd had his five-minute warning.

'Just another five minutes,' he pleaded: slurred and resonant. He always wants five minutes more, then more again.

'No, come on now, love,' persisted Evie, trying to stay jolly but firm.

'I want more.'

After a while Evie had to prise the controller from

his fingers.

The screaming started: 'I hate you.' It got louder and tears of anger dribbled down William's cheeks. Evie turned off the computer and left him to simmer down after trying unsuccessfully to reason with him for fifteen minutes. She tried to stay calm, peeling carrots and washing mushrooms, as the onions sizzled in a pan on the stove. She was cooking the tea. He carried on shouting for another twenty minutes, then he shouted, 'Okay, I'll strangle myself then'.

'Well, watch you don't hurt yourself, love,' said Evie. He was in the kitchen now and he put his hands around his throat, and he screamed so much it seemed he wouldn't catch his breath. She lifted the lid, to look at the onions, spitting and beginning to blacken now, though she hardly noticed. We have a lot of meals with a charred character about them! 'You won't go on the computer tomorrow if you carry on.' But it made no difference.

'I'm going to destroy the house,' he yelled, and he rammed the kitchen table with his wheelchair. But his arms aren't strong and he couldn't cause any damage. Most of our furniture is pretty battered anyway.

Evie looked up as if she hadn't heard. 'Careful, love, or you might scratch the table.' Without waiting for his reply she offered to put on a story tape, or get his Star Wars figures. 'What about *The Hobbit?* You haven't listened to that for a while.'

'I hate you,' he screamed. Tears and mucous mingled and dripped. Evie left the cooker and cleaned him up till her hankie was damp from wiping.

Eventually his temper subsided, and later they hugged each other and he sobbed like a baby. She felt his ribs through his sweater as she held him on her knee, and so wished he was able to wreck the house.

'Sorry, Mum.'

'It's okay now, love.'

Later, at tea time, Robbie held up a forkful of pasta.

'Why do you always burn the onions, mum?' he asked.

Evie gave him a wounded glance.

'Shut up, big ears,' snapped William.

'Now, William. . .' I said, giving him a warning look.

2

Why?

The notion of adoption has been around for a long time. The first recorded instance is when Miriam found Moses floating around in those bulrushes. These days, children get adopted for all kinds of reasons. They may be orphaned, unwanted, neglected, abused or abandoned. The thing they have in common of course is that they all need parents. Various people come forward for various reasons. Step-parents adopt their partners' children to confirm family commitments, and grandparents and other relatives take over when parents can't cope or are ill or die. But on the whole, it is childless couples who go in search of children, sometimes travelling to orphanages half way around the world in a quest to make their lives complete; to form families and to fulfil yearnings for parenthood. Usually the search is for a baby, or if that is not manageable (fewer and fewer babies are available for adoption anywhere in the world), for a child as young as possible, and one as perfect as possible, in terms of health and development. It's hard to say why anyone would actively search for a child with disabilities to adopt, and what the motivation might be.

I thought long and hard before deciding to write this

story. We're just an ordinary family of six, who, like thousands of others, happen to have a child with disabilities. And he just happens to be adopted. We'd prefer to be more private about that, but it's a bit difficult because William was nearly four when he joined our family, and of course in a small town everyone knows everyone's business, and William soon lets strangers know all about his adoptive status. Evie and I are not perfect parents, in fact we're very flawed – we have made lots of mistakes with all our children: we nag, lose our tempers, make them feel guilty about things, over-protect them, under-protect them, don't give them enough time or give them too much attention. Given all this, it feels a bit presumptuous to tell our story. So why go more public than we need to? I suppose it's because we think that on the whole ours is a positive story of adoption (so far) for the whole family, and we believe adoption is the best option for many children who can't stay with their families. There are thousands of children in the UK waiting for adoption, and many will never be placed with families. I hope that by sharing our experience we may be able to offer a bit of practical advice and insight to others who might be thinking of adoption, and in particular, if they are thinking of adopting a child with disabilities. William and the rest of the children know I'm writing this book, and to protect them, and William's birth family, to whom I'd hate to cause any distress, I've changed everyone's names.

The people who know that William is adopted fall into three camps: those who know, but never mention it, which is the majority of our friends; those who regard us as saints, which is very squirm-inducing; and those who think we are off our heads. It's now over six years since William came to live with us. William is our son, just as much as if we'd seen him distend Evie's belly in pregnancy as the others before him had done, and just as much as if we'd cared for him since birth and through those early, missing years. Just the same as the others, but different too, because of all he brought with him and will carry with him, always.

We made our first phone call to the adoption society about seven years ago. At that time our three birth children, Ed, Kate and Robbie, were aged thirteen, eleven and ten. Life was good. We didn't *need* any more children. We certainly didn't plan to have any more birth children; Evie had had the operation! If you pause to think about it, why does anyone want children anyway, whether through birth or adoption? Parents sacrifice careers, nights out, holidays, material things, freedom and so on, in return for years of thankless exhaustion. It probably has its roots in an instinctive drive to keep the species going, to preserve the family name, and an innate need to be needed. Our lives would have been emptier, I think, if we had not had the joy and angst of helping our children grow up, from the earliest stages of utter dependency after the cutting of the actual umbilical cord, to the gradual severing of the metaphorical cord as they approach adulthood. Not that it ever gets completely cut, of course. Parenthood is a lifelong life-choice for those lucky enough to be able to make it. But it's not what everyone wants, which is fine, and for some it is unlooked for.

We lived, and still do, in a small Scottish town, and as our three children were getting older, my wife, Evie, and I were beginning to have a bit more time to ourselves. Not that life has ever been quiet: my work as a social worker, and Evie's job as a community development worker and volunteer means that, for as long as I can remember, we've always had a backlog of cleaning, decorating, gardening, and piles of unsorted papers spilling out from various dusty corners, which we call "the in-tray". We'll catch up one day: one evening or one weekend, or one holiday or maybe when we retire. Or maybe we won't ever catch up: life's too short to fritter it away on hoovering!

So why did we make that phone call? And why did we

make it then, seven years ago, when life was getting a bit easier? It wasn't just so that we could continue to have an excuse for not doing the hoovering! As anyone who has been through an adoption assessment process knows, the hoover gets used more before the social worker's visits than ever before. The reasons are difficult to explain, and probably impossible for anyone else to understand, but I think we made the call when we did, precisely because life was good. We were sitting in the garden one sunny spring weekend; the grass had been cut, the sparrows hopped and chattered, sunshine spilled and moved across the distant hills, and the freshly ground coffee was perfect. After a fairly short conversation, we agreed that I would phone the adoption society on the Monday. Our three children were all out and the house was very quiet. We were surprisingly decisive.

Evie and I had talked about adoption for years as something we might do some day. The seed of the idea had lain dormant, but like something stored in a matchbox, we took it out and re-examined it periodically. In my work I was involved in planning for children in need of adoption, and was aware that some would never get families; mostly older children with traumatic histories, sibling groups and children with additional needs and disabilities. I regularly saw adoption magazines, with pages and pages of groomed, smiling children, coaxed into appealing poses by professional photographers, to catch the eye of would-be families, with positively spun captions underneath:

> *Alfie has had lots of changes in his life. He has a cheeky personality and needs lots of patience and firm boundaries.*

Being in the business, I knew that probably meant a history of abuse, attachment disorder and ADHD (Attention Deficit Hyperactive Disorder). Half jokingly at first, I'd spoken with Evie about how instead of spending our working lives shuffling bits of paper around, we'd be better doing something that would make a real difference, but we didn't do anything other than talk about it till after that sunny weekend.

We'd enjoyed being parents, and compared to many had had an easy time of it. Both Evie and I had travelled the world a bit when we were younger; we both did voluntary service overseas, took risks with our lives and enjoyed our freedom. We'd settled down together comparatively late; we were in our mid-thirties when we got married. Ed was born just before our first wedding anniversary, to the jubilation of our parents; my mother had nearly given up hope of having grandchildren. We had moved into a large Edinburgh flat six weeks earlier, which we had bought cheap because of the state it was in: an elderly pipe smoker had lived in it for thirty years and droplets of brown, sticky nicotine deposits hung from the ornate cornices like little stalactites. We discovered the magical properties of sugar soap, and with the help of friends and my dad got the place just about habitable before Ed arrived. The plumber was bleeding the newly installed central heating radiators as Evie's waters broke. The temperature in the flat rose as the frequency of her contractions increased!

We were all ready. We'd read all the books about foetal development; we'd been to the National Childbirth Trust classes; I'd learned how to comfort Evie during labour; I'd invested in an expensive natural sponge to moisten her lips when the going got tough; and I'd got the portable cassette player and the tape of Puccini arias lined up to greet the arrival of the baby. We'd decided against an amniocentesis test because of the risk, and because we'd agreed that we'd have the baby whatever the outcome of the test might be anyway. After her waters broke I gave Evie some curry I'd re-hydrated out of a packet to keep her going, and we went off to the hospital by taxi. We'd hoped for a home birth and changed doctors to one who was supportive, but the health authorities would have none of it because of Evie's status as an "elderly primagravida" (first time middle-aged mother), a label she deeply resented.

At the hospital Evie's contractions came at regular intervals, but the cervix didn't dilate and we wearied of Puccini. Nothing much happened for hours. Then, suddenly, Evie brought the curry back up (she's never forgiven me for insisting she should have something to eat), the contractions came rapidly, Puccini fell silent, and Evie apologised to everyone for everything; she's always been needlessly apologetic for things she has absolutely no control over. A doctor performed an episiotomy and Ed arrived. Evie had to be stitched and cleaned up. I remember cascades of blood, and Ed had to be rushed off for suction in case he'd swallowed some of his own faeces in his struggle down the canal. I tried to make myself useful by rather feebly utilising the expensive sponge on Evie's lips, till Ed was brought back in and handed to me. Miriam Stoppard said in her book, which we'd read, that skin-to-skin contact was important, so I held him against my cheek. When I pulled him away he looked around the room wide eyed and silent – one of the most special moments of my life – before I handed him to Evie. We went home the next day and were soon invaded by waves of grandparents and aunts and uncles. Adoption is a bit different, but I'll get to that later...

Twenty-two months later, Kate arrived. We had a "Domino" delivery: domiciliary in and out. My dad had been staying with us when Evie's waters broke. We told him that the baby was on its way, but he didn't seem to believe us. He was a bit more attentive when we went off to the hospital in the taxi, but was plainly stupefied when we came back before breakfast the next morning with his granddaughter, just as he was helping Ed to clean his teeth. The memorable thing about Kate's actual birth was that the midwife thought she detected another heartbeat in Evie's womb after she was born, and believed it might be an undiagnosed twin. My immediate thought was, how were we going to transport three tiny children around in our Morris Minor! The midwife pressed the alarm button and the birthing room filled with doctors and nurses, but the "heartbeat" turned out to be the placenta pulsating.

Robbie was born eighteen months later. The grandparents seemed a little less enthusiastic about the prospect of his arrival. After all, we'd got one of each already! Three children under the age of four seemed to Evie's mum a bit excessive. The next few years were certainly fairly busy. We had a double buggy, which skinned the heels of countless pedestrians, and the logistics of shepherding the three children around and going to activities and on holidays was a bit of a challenge. There were the playgroups, nurseries and later on the schools to get to. There were the childhood illnesses to survive.

All five of us had the same tummy bug at one point and then Robbie had a mysterious virus and was hospitalised for a week. Evie and I took turns staying with him in the hospital. At one point he seemed to be fading away – one of the lowlights of my life – but he rallied and came home. He brought chicken pox with him, even though he'd been in an isolation room, and soon the others caught it – spots everywhere and crying for days on end. But the three of them were good friends with each other when they were little, and as I say, we had it easy. Despite the ups and downs we really enjoyed being parents. So that was another reason for thinking of adoption: we enjoyed being parents.

The decision to adopt, or even to make that first phone call, isn't at all straightforward. It's the beginning of an unknown journey. I've always been a slightly nervous traveller. I like to know exactly what the arrangements are and to get to the airport in plenty of time. But the adoption journey is more of a mystery tour. There was no child in mind when we embarked on the process. It's a bit like deciding to get married without having a specific partner in mind. Of course, having a birth child is also like that, but the birth child grows out of you, and you make that skin-to-skin contact in the first few moments. An adopted child already has a name, has come from the union of others and has a personality and a will that is partly formed. He or she might have had that special skin-to-skin contact with someone else, if they were lucky.

We thought a lot about the sort of child that would fit in best with our family. We felt there needed to be a substantial age gap between Robbie and the newcomer, so as to avoid too much rivalry and minimise the risk of Robbie feeling displaced. We planned that the new child would share a room with Robbie. We had a little box room, which was used as a "study"; in other words, we kept our "in tray" and miscellaneous junk in it. If possible we wanted to hang on to it – but it could always be used as a bedroom if the need arose. We were wary of taking on a child with acute attachment difficulties, or one with overt sexualised behaviour, because of our protectiveness towards the others.

We ended up thinking that a child with mild disabilities might be the best fit: perhaps a child with Down's syndrome or a limited physical disability. We'd each done a bit of voluntary work with disabled children in the past, and had provided a little bit of care to the disabled child of some friends. The summer before, Evie had met a man at the Great Yorkshire Show who, along with his wife, had adopted four children with Down's syndrome, all adults by then. Two of them were with him. Evie got chatting – she comes from a long line of chatterers – and came away inspired at the man's life choice and the richness that had followed for him and his wife and children. All these little experiences added up and influenced the way we would go.

Of course, the term "mild disability" is a bit elastic. As a prospective birth parent your first thought at the birth is whether the baby is okay. As an actual parent you never know what lies ahead: there's the possibility of impaired health or development; the spectre of your children being drawn to drugs, drink, getting into trouble or into relationships that worry you. If disabilities are detected at birth, there's the added uncertainty of how independent or otherwise children might become. In the case of William, whom we adopted, a major concern was whether or not he would be able to walk. He's ten years old now, and we think the answer is no. But the prospects were brighter when he was placed with us.

Then there was the question as to whether we should foster or adopt. We never really considered fostering. We both felt that if children didn't have a birth family they could stay with for ever, then adoption was the next best thing, and that we were most likely to make a real difference to a child if we committed wholly through adoption. Having said that, there are many children with disabilities who do very well in long-term foster placements, and of course for children who have significant contact with their birth families, that is often the preferred option. We'd talked to the other children before that first phone call. We were always clear we could not go ahead without their support. We'd talked in general terms about children who needed families, and engendered some excitement and enthusiasm, which we hoped would not be disappointed. We kept stressing that it might not happen; that we might decide not to go ahead; that we might not be approved and so on. But a momentum developed after that first phone call that led to William joining our family a few months later.

3

On paper and in reality

We decided to approach a small Catholic adoption agency. As a social worker in a local authority, I had an overview of the local agencies that were around, and we felt most comfortable dealing with a small specialist agency. I phoned up on the Monday and had an informal chat with one of the social workers. He arranged to send out some information and a form to fill in if we wanted to ask for an initial visit. The form duly came and we completed it and returned it the next weekend. By that stage, our interest had solidified and we'd psyched ourselves up to go forward seriously. I think it was about a month before a social worker was able to come and see us. This is a blink of an eye from the perspective of the agency, but felt like a very long time from our point of view as prospective adopters.

The initial visit seemed to go well. It must be awful for social workers to deal with adoptive applicants who are also social workers and who might think they know it all. And whilst *I* know we are the most normal family on the planet, some of the information we presented must have given her a sinking feeling:

'No, we don't have a telly. Yes, we're a busy family –

Sundays are usually taken up getting our daughter into town (25 miles away) because she sings in the cathedral choir both in the morning and afternoon. Yes, our parents are all getting on and have some health worries. Yes, we're getting on too! Yes, Evie is vegetarian. Yes, we are aware that statistically speaking the rate of adoption breakdown is greater for children who are adopted into families who already have birth children...'

The social worker shifted about in one of our old armchairs; a horsehair-filled heirloom with wayward springs, that looks good but isn't at all comfortable. She tried to make a surreptitious note, while grappling with coffee in our best china, complete with saucer, and a crumbling square of Evie's flapjack. I still wonder if she wrote "lunatic fringe" in her notebook. It's an interesting process being interviewed about personal things. We found ourselves being very open and enjoyed talking indulgently, in detail, about ourselves. Not that the first visit went into much detail; it was more about describing the process of group preparation, home-study and matching. We talked about our interest in adopting a child with mild disabilities, trying to explain why we felt this would probably fit best with the needs, ages and stages of the other children. As we said it, we knew we had to think this through a bit more...

We were lucky in the timing of our application to the adoption society because a preparation group for would-be applicants was about to start and we were invited to join. It meant weekly evening sessions in the city. Evie and I would meet there after work. We had to arrange childcare, of course, which meant we began telling a few friends what we were doing. Most thought we were crazy. They, like us, were at the stage where the end was almost in sight – those exhausting years of anxiety-ridden child care were drawing to a slow but inevitable conclusion. And the notion of taking on a child with disabilities, even mild disabilities, was outside rational thought.

There were half a dozen couples and a single person in the preparation group. Except for us, all were childless. Over the seven weeks of group preparation we had input about child development, attachment issues, birth families, contact and managing challenging behaviour. We felt a bit self-conscious in the group, as I'm sure everyone did, and it took a week or two before I confessed to being a social worker with quite a bit of experience in placing children for adoption as well as assessing and training adopters. I really didn't want to set myself up as an expert – this needed to be a personal exploration for us and our family – but it was tricky wearing the right hat at the right time. Another thing that made us self-conscious was the fact that we had three children and were looking for another; this set us apart. We were at pains to explain, during the coffee breaks, that we were specifically interested in a child with disabilities, almost wanting to reassure the others that we were not rivals for the sort of children they might be interested in. Their reaction was either admiration, which made us cringe, or no reaction at all, which we interpreted as folk thinking we were a bit odd.

The group was enjoyable, and we managed to keep up with the homework we were given and to get to all the sessions. It's interesting how easy it is to get into a mindset of feeling you have to prove something, though. This was a process for helping us to decide whether or not to go ahead, but both the groups and the home study inevitably have an element of being judged, and of course, whenever we are judged, we want to perform well, perhaps rather more than honestly.

There was very little in the group sessions about children with disabilities. There was lots of discussion about children with learning difficulties but not about those with physical impairments. The agency did not place many children with disabilities and tended to explore these notions during home studies. It's very difficult to think of children in the abstract and we found it hard to know what sort of child would best fit in with our family. The assessment form we were later given had a long list of childhood conditions and disabilities – which could we accept? We ticked as appropriate, but that gave very little feel for how a child might be. Down's syndrome: tick; sexualised behaviour; cross; child born of incestuous relationship: tick; child without speech: maybe. It all felt a bit random.

We turned to the adoption magazines and looked at the sad little profiles there. It sounds awful: like leafing through an Argos catalogue, trying to find the right consumer durable, but it brought the reality much closer for us. In fact, before the group process was complete, we read about a child who seemed just right: a little boy with albinism (inherited lack of pigmentation of the skin) and a skin condition and mild developmental delay. There was a photograph and a positive narrative, and we kept going back to his brief details time and again, building up our own picture, largely fantasy I'm sure, as to what he would be like. In the end we went with our feelings and phoned the adoption agency (we didn't have an allocated worker at that stage) and mentioned our interest. All cart before horse stuff, and not really the done thing, but we felt that this was our life and we needed to take charge; to do nothing might be to let an opportunity slip forever.

Our agency was surprisingly supportive, and made contact with the child's social worker. The child was right down in the south of England. The profile had sparked a lot of enquiries. They kept a note of our interest, but after a time the child was matched with an approved family and that was that. Having dipped our toe into this unconventional approach, we carried on with it, and after a few more weeks spotted four-year-old William's profile:

William is a delightful, happy toddler with an engaging personality who is beginning to assert his independence.

He is sociable, and thrives on the company of other children and on adult attention. He loves swimming, water play and animals. William has cerebral palsy, which mainly affects his mobility. He requires daily physiotherapy and ongoing medical support, and is likely to need a walking aid. William is responding well to the stimulation provided by the children's centre he is attending and has made excellent progress in the foster family he has lived with for the last two-and-a-half years. He has a good attachment to his carer who describes him as a rewarding child to care for.

William is of white parentage and needs a white adoptive family, either a couple or a single carer. Letterbox contact is planned with his birth family and two younger brothers, who are to be adopted separately. He is freed for adoption. An adoption allowance may be payable.

* * *

There was a picture of a very normal-looking little boy with eyes shining red, caught by the flash of the camera. The picture hadn't been taken by a professional photographer. We read the details over and over, till we'd learned them by heart, and looked at the picture again and again. Another call to the agency. By this time, we had an allocated social worker and she agreed to make enquiries. After a few days, she got back to us to say that William was still "available" – in fact, he'd been waiting for a while. She gave us a bit more information and, on the strength of that, we decided that we would like to be seriously considered. We were told that William lived in Scotland, and the impression conveyed in the magazine, that his needs were largely related to mobility problems, was confirmed.

For the next several months, William was a theoretical feature of our family. The only information we had of him was a couple of paragraphs and the smiling photograph with the red eyes. He developed in our minds, but in a way that was inevitably quite different to the real child. Meantime we continued with the home study. We filled in various parts of forms and had a series of interviews with the social worker, usually as a couple, but also separately. She interviewed the children, at that time aged fourteen, twelve and ten. By this time we'd talked to them in detail about the prospect of adoption, and we'd told them about the kind of child we might adopt and mentioned William as a possibility. They seemed positive about the idea. They quickly developed a sense of compassion for him and for children like him, but like us, probably built up their own fantasies. We talked with them about the downsides of adoption – restrictions in the things we would be able to do and the demands another child would make on our time. They were able to voice a bit of apprehension, but my abiding memory of their reaction is that they trusted us to make decisions that would be right for us all. That gave us the green light but it felt like a big responsibility.

Eventually the forms were completed and signed and there was another wait for the adoption panel. In time we found ourselves in a room with about half a dozen panel members, along with our social worker and the agency medical advisor. It was a bit like an interview, though the idea of us attending was meant to enable us to experience the process openly and not be subjected to a Spanish Inquisition. We've always been a little paranoid, and of course no matter how open the process tries to be, people will talk about you in private, and it is inevitable to wonder what they really think of you. However, the process was relatively painless, and we were recommended for approval. We received our letter from the agency decision-maker a few days later and it was all systems go.

Over the next few weeks we were given lots more information about William. His social worker, Helen, came to see us – another inspection of us as a family. No one else was interested in adopting William, despite national publicity. This felt like good news in a sense, but was also a pressure. No other families. What if we decided he was not for us?

Helen knew William well, having been his social worker for most of his life. She knew his family and his younger two siblings who had just been placed for adoption. She helped to bring him alive for us. He was beginning to string short sentences together; he was very sociable; he could be wilful; he had feeding difficulties; he could walk with an aid and minimum support; he had regular appointments at hospital for Botox injections to help prevent his hamstrings from tightening. He was very settled in his foster placement and moving to a new family would be traumatic, but his carers did not feel able to make a permanent commitment. Helen left us with a video of William in action: pushing himself around garden paths on a little wooden trike; playing in the swimming pool; having physiotherapy; in his standing frame; eating custard (which was to become a big feature of his early weeks with us). She also left us with yet another form, giving details of his history: ten weeks premature; drugs withdrawal at birth; the first three months almost alone in hospital with a team of nurses and doctors; the unfurling diagnosis of cerebral palsy. But despite all this he came across as a positive, gutsy little boy, and we began to admire him.

We thought about it for a few days and said we were still interested. We then met his foster carer, who gave graphic details of what he was like to live with. He obviously took up nearly all her time. Feeding was a big problem – he had to be given all sorts of liquid food supplements, which had to be spooned into him – he ate very little on a voluntary basis; he was frequently sick, he was below the third centile in terms of size, head circumference and weight. He had lots of hospital appointments; he had a place in a special day nursery for infants with disabilities. It felt less positive. He did have a cheery disposition, but could be wilful. We wondered if we were up to it, and whether this was what we really wanted. We began to agonise. We were getting a picture of a more needy child than we had envisaged. After lots of discussion we still found it difficult to know what to do, but having got this far – he'd been in our thoughts for months by this time – we decided to keep going.

The next step was to meet the community paediatrician, the head of the special nursery and the hospital consultant. The paediatrician produced fat, dog-eared, buff coloured files and let us look through them over mugs of coffee in a bleak little room. She then went over William's history with us and answered our questions openly and honestly. There was a phrase in the file describing him as "cortically blind"; the first reference we had seen to any visual impairment. She assembled information about this for us: William has nystagmus (involuntary eye movements) and finds it difficult to focus, particularly on moving objects. He has no depth perception and is cortically visually impaired, although he has learnt many coping strategies.

We became aware of the gaps in his experience of being parented, despite the full and very supportive package that was in place. He was a "corporately parented" child. This ghastly term was invented to stress that the responsibility for "looked after" children (children in care as they used to be called) rests not with one department but with the whole council, and others besides in Health and Education. Whilst the notion of corporate responsibility for children is excellent in some ways, if you stop and think about it, it is a bizarre way to consider bringing up children. What children need are parents to fight for them, to argue for their needs and to be a thorn in the side of those who do not have their interests at heart. In other words: Real Parents. William had been lucky in that he'd had the same social worker throughout his life, and had lived with one carer for the last three years. Other children have multiple placements, carers and social workers, and no one in their lives who really knows them, let alone who will fight for them. And even in William's case, with his relatively stable progress in care, no one really had a detailed knowledge of his needs or a single-minded determination to make sure they would be met. An American therapist, Vera Fahlberg, talks of the need for children in care to have an 'irrational advocate': someone who will fight on their behalf, even though they might be a nuisance or might be wrong. The important thing for children is to have someone on their side, and to know it. In William's case, pieces of information got mislaid, like the visual impairment, which in the scheme of things might seem fairly minor, but which, as time has passed, has become a bigger and bigger feature of his life.

The neurologist was obviously quite suspicious of our interest in William – another one who couldn't quite work us out. He quizzed us about what we knew about cerebral palsy (CP), and rubbed his eyes almost wearily as he explained the basics. The messages from William's brain to the various parts of his body didn't work well. He had involuntary spasms; he had a programme of medication to keep the effects of CP at bay, but would probably need more invasive surgery in the future. His life expectancy would be normal. It was impossible to say how mobile he would become or whether he might become independent. He was microcephalic (his head was too small) and would be intellectually limited, but he was making good progress. And so on.

The more information we got the more apprehensive we became. We had sleepless nights. Could we make this lifelong commitment? Would we manage? Would we have a life of our own at all? William seemed more disabled than we had anticipated and we hesitated and agonised and talked and talked. But none of that really helped to clarify things. There he was, about twenty-five miles away, waiting for a family and it didn't feel as if there was anyone who could help us to make a decision. At the end of the day it was a lifestyle choice that only we could work out. We did discuss our mixed feelings with our social worker, but to a limited degree, partly because it had to be our decision and partly, maybe, because we didn't want to lose face, which sounds a stupid thing looking back, but I think adopters, having gone through all the tests and assessments, get to the stage where they have a lot to lose. It felt as if the social worker disapproved of our uncertainty, but whether this was really the case or a function of our paranoia wasn't clear.

We decided to go for it, though we were still apprehensive. We'd take a risk. We'd got this far. Yes it would be hard work. We looked again at the videos and pored over the details. Behind all the labels he was a little boy in need of a family, and we knew it would be difficult but decided we'd cope. Still, we had the collywobbles and even when we phoned our social worker to say we'd like to proceed, we had doubts.

Before we could begin to be introduced to William we had to be formally "matched" with him by the adoption panel of the local authority where he lived. This meant another wait of a few weeks till a date came up. We weren't invited to this panel. Our social worker represented us and members of the panel had all our papers and William's papers. The match was agreed and a co-ordinator was appointed to make arrangements for introductions and William's ultimate move to come and live with us. At this stage, in theory at least, it would still have been possible to pull out. In fact we could have pulled out at any time, even after he was placed with us. Christmas was approaching and it was decided to wait until after Christmas before starting the introductions, because of all the emotions that are around at Christmas and the false, tinselly atmosphere.

Meanwhile, we were in the throes of having a

conservatory built, so part of the house was being demolished and the garden was full of piles of ripped out timber and rubble. We were also busy decorating (a rare event for us – the previous time was when we had burst pipes which brought ceilings down a few years earlier). William was to share a room with Robbie. Robbie chose a frieze of leaping dolphins and we emulsioned the walls, gloss-painted the woodwork, had a new carpet fitted and got some fresh curtains. We bought a cot-bed for William and painted up a wardrobe and chest of drawers to house his things.

Christmas came and went, with the usual visits to both sets of parents. We were able to give them a fair bit of information about William, and, to our faces at least, they were supportive. Our first contact with William was scheduled to begin a couple of days after Christmas.

Evie and I made the first trip to the foster carers' house together one Saturday. We'd met Janet, the female carer before – a confident, competent woman – and she greeted us warmly at the door and showed us into the living room. William was sitting in a special chair, meant to help his posture. He had a little table in front of him and was playing with some toy trains. He turned as we came into the room and said, 'Hello Mum and Dad'. He was all smiles. He'd been prepared for the meeting; it was plain he was going to adopt us! We'd made him a small album of photos of us and given it to his social worker who had passed it on to William: The Marsden Family. Each photo had a caption such as: 'Here are Ed, Kate, Robbie and Mum on holiday, camping – Dad isn't in the picture – he's taking the photo.' The album was on his little table, alongside his Thomas the Tank engines. Ed had drawn a picture of Thomas on the inside cover of the album. William had memorised the contents.

We spent an hour or so with him, playing with his trains and having simple conversations about Christmas and so on. We'd bought him a present: a speaking book about Thomas the tank engine. He wasn't very impressed. He had an extensive collection of Thomas paraphernalia and this was a very modest addition to it. The carer acted as interpreter and go between. William was interested in my beard and wanted to touch it. In fact, at that first meeting he seemed drawn to me rather than Evie, but only through this superficial fascination. He stayed in his chair the whole time.

Evie and I debriefed on the way home. It wasn't love at first sight. We'd somehow assumed that any doubts would vaporise like lifting mist, but it wasn't so. It was really hard to imagine him as ours. But then, we reasoned it would be a bit odd in some ways if it felt he was ours from the outset, though we'd heard stories of other adopters who'd known at first sight that "this was it". Trying to talk about it rationally, there was nothing after the visit that, logically, should have put us off, but I think we'd both been hoping that the first meeting would dispel all our doubts, and it hadn't happened like that.

More agonising, more discussions with the social worker and more efforts to be rational in the most irrational of situations. We decided to carry on with more introductions. We had a hectic programme of visits to the foster carers' home, usually together but sometimes separately. We began helping with feeding and bathing, and experienced mild temper tantrums at bedtime. We took the other children to see him; they all seemed much more positive than we felt! Then we took him out for the first time – a trip to the museum – and had responsibility for getting some lunch into him – a baked potato if I remember rightly. It was a slow business but generally seemed to go well, and William seemed relaxed with us.

Our ambivalence continued, but we began to feel more certain that we wanted to go ahead. We had more outings with the other children – a trip to the zoo, then later a trip to the city farm. William seemed very taken with Ed, Kate and Robbie, and they thought he was great. That encouraged us. We tried to work out for ourselves how much mobility he had. He used an ordinary buggy at that stage and couldn't stand or walk, but he could do a walking action if he was held under both arms, and his legs seemed quite strong. He could commando crawl, but not go on his hands and knees. He was very sociable, but slightly in a world of his own. He asked lots of questions, but didn't always answer questions put to him. He had clear speech, apart from a few problems articulating "th" and "f" and he had a fair vocabulary – better than we'd been led to believe.

It was pretty obvious that William would be hard work. He was more physically disabled than we'd envisaged, but on the positive side he seemed to get on with the other children and they liked him. I think after all those months of thinking about a hypothetical child, it was a relief to have a real one in front of them and not one who seemed as needy as we'd maybe led them to expect. This was very reassuring. We still worried that we didn't love him straight away, but then tried to think sensibly about that – it would be ludicrous to expect us to. Every time we saw him he'd say, 'Hello Mum and Dad' and 'Goodbye Mum and Dad,' and he was already talking about his new brothers and sister. There was no turning back.

4

What have we done?

When William first joined us it was a bit like being parents for the first time again – having a being who is totally dependent on you, despite your utter lack of experience and skills. Our knowledge of William was based only on theory. We were the sort of parents who'd used muslin and towelling nappies with our babies, and washed them in vinegar (the nappies, not the children!), in the confident hope, even then, that it might save the planet. I'd learned to fold nappies using the "origami" method and to tuck them into the plastic pants. Evie was always far better than I – her nappies were a comfortable joy for our babies. Mine were always a bit lumpy and skewed, and tended to leak. But the babies had all snuggled up in our arms and taken Evie's milk, and after a while we grew in confidence and it all came right.

William wasn't a baby, and he wasn't ours, at least not at first. We learned the new skills needed to care for him fairly quickly, but the emotional bonding came much later. Without doubt, for the first two years or so the emotional challenges he presented to us as parents were far greater than the demands of his physical disability. In fact these were a doddle by comparison. The balance shifted as he grew older, and now that he's our son – fully ours – and sees us as his parents, the physical and wider social demands are the most worrying and challenging, and the emotional ones, though always there, as for any child, are the more manageable.

When the great day finally arrived, we collected William in two cars. We'd bought a seven seater in anticipation of his arrival, but had to move his entire past with him: all his toys, clothes, photograph albums and equipment, and so needed the two cars. We didn't linger long at the foster carers' house. William had lived there for nearly three years and it was heart wrenching for all concerned. None of us wanted to prolong the agony. William travelled in one car with the other children, and me at the wheel. The others distracted him, so that he chatted and sang songs with them, though he kept mentioning Aunty Janet, and asking when he would see her again. Evie came on behind, her car laden with suitcases, equipment and bin bags full of toys.

Once we were home we got everything unloaded and took William for an exploratory tour of the house. He'd visited a couple of times, so it was fairly familiar. The alterations still weren't finished, so it was also a bit chaotic. We were excited, but anxious, and it was a case of getting through the day more than anything else. We played with him together or taking turns – the children were all very good – and later we had tea together. At that time he was on various custards and food supplements, as well as baby food and liquidised food. The only thing he drank was milk. It took ages to coax something in to him and he really ate very little. Then we carried him upstairs for his bath and he went to bed in his new cot, surrounded by his enormous collection of cuddly toys, which effectively buried him. We read him various stories, about Thomas the Tank Engine, of course, and said goodnight several times. Janet had written down all sorts of tips and advice about routines, meal times, how he might play up and techniques that calmed him down, and we tried to follow them, but of course they didn't work. William desperately missed his own room and everything that was familiar. He took ages to settle, calling for us, for Aunty Janet, and for Robbie, who was sharing his room. He cried, he wanted to go "home," but eventually he went to sleep, sobbing intermittently, beyond comfort. We were exhausted, and after only about six hours!

It's impossible to know what William really felt in those early days. When Evie's dad died about three years ago after a long illness, during which we'd had time to prepare, it was like some part of you had gone missing and could not be replaced. When Ed and Kate left home to go to university, Evie and I had an aching feeling of loss and anxiety, and a sad sense of things ending. When I went on Voluntary Service Overseas all those years ago, leaving everything I knew behind, I had a feeling of fear, apprehension and finality, even though it was to be for only two years. And we were all able to talk with others about these losses and changes, and work them out to a degree. Poor William had limited vocabulary; no friends or adults he could fully trust; just the raw aching emotions of fear, loss, loneliness and anger.

William woke early next day (Sunday). He called out from his room: 'I want my Aunty Janet!' Evie and I lay in bed, almost overwhelmed by the problems that lay ahead for the next few hours, never mind the next twenty years and more! We felt compassion for William at that stage; it would be a case of hanging on and doing the job of parents as well as we could, and hoping that love would come in time and that it would be reciprocated.

It's amazing how quickly you can feel de-skilled and out of your depth. Of course we knew that William was experiencing real loss; he had been taken away from the person to whom he related as a mother, and he was devastated. He didn't want us and he showed it. We distracted him for short periods and the children played with him. He showed an interest in our dog, Molly, who just growled at this new arrival who she thought was clearly below her in the pecking order. Every few minutes he wanted Aunty Janet, no matter what we did. It was hard not to take it personally. Later, on that first full day, Evie had to take Kate to the cathedral so she could sing in the two services. William and the boys and I got through the day, playing together with his toys, watching videos, eating and nappy-changing. At one point I took him to the supermarket in his buggy and he made it very clear, when I was half way down the shopping list, that he'd had enough. He began crying and screaming and demanding to go home. I cut short the shopping trip, but he cried all the way home. Passers-by turned their heads and looked concerned. We met a friend halfway and I introduced them, but William just screamed and screamed. She phoned later to check that I was all right. No matter how much we tried to understand how William felt, it was hard to react rationally, and on one level it felt as if we'd brought a monster into the family.

Those first few days were hard work, physically, and very difficult emotionally. On the second day he developed a heavy cold; probably brought on by the emotional trauma. I had some adoption leave from work, and it was a full time job for the two of us to care for William. I had serious doubts about whether we could make it work – it exposed my own shortcomings as a person, particularly my own emotional vulnerability, in a way that was very hard to talk about, even with Evie at the time; she was more stoic.

There were no plans for William to see Aunty Janet for the first few weeks. The theory was that contact too early would unsettle him and make it harder for him to bond with us. I still don't know whether early contact with Janet would have reassured or unsettled him. It would undoubtedly have eased his pain for a time, but maybe only for him to have to go through it all again. As it was, when she did visit after about six weeks or so he was thrilled, but it took about two days for him to get back to "normal" again. During those two days he told us he didn't want to stay with us any more or be adopted and that he didn't like us. He wasn't able to articulate it quite in those terms, but through his limited speech, his unresponsiveness to all that we tried, and his physical rejection of us, as far as his strength allowed, he made his feelings very clear. He was so inconsolable that in the end, on day two, Evie laid him on the floor, surrounded by his cuddly toys, which had the familiar smell and memory of Aunty Janet, and left him to cry and grieve alone for a while.

Janet visited periodically for the first two years or so and each time he was grief-stricken for a day or two when she left, and made it very clear to us that he would rather stay with her than be part of our family.

At the same time as trying to manage all this emotionally draining grief, we were trying to get competent at dealing with William's physical needs. He was a very small boy, and at that time our backs had not yet gone, so it was fairly easy to carry him about, but we had to get used to lifting him in a way that was comfortable for us all. We had to re-learn the art of nappy-changing (I'm afraid we abandoned high principles in favour of ease, and bought disposable nappies in bulk), the technique of putting him in his special chair and his standing frame, and doing physiotherapy – stretching exercises mainly on his legs.

The most difficult job was making sure William ate enough. It took about an hour-and-a-half of patient spooning to get a reasonable amount of food into him, and then more often than not he would bring it all back up in spectacular fashion! The best technique was to distract him with a video of the dreaded Thomas, and sneak the food into him. I still think of custard and vomit when I hear that jingle and Ringo Starr's voiceover – William became conditioned to opening his mouth like a fledgling sparrow as the spoon approached. We all ate together as a family as a rule, so meal times got a bit disrupted by this new ritual.

The feeding difficulties were attributed to the cerebral palsy – involuntary muscular spasms – but we suspected that they were also caught up with emotional factors. Evie tasted the food supplements and found them disgusting. She's always been a slightly obsessive advocate of the organic cause, and decided to try and bring some nutritional value and enjoyment to meal times for William. So over the next few weeks and months we experimented with finger foods and small portions of the food the rest of the family ate, and it worked! Mealtimes were still slow; he still had to have it pushed into his mouth, but the regurgitating eased and he began putting on weight. After a few months he was no longer below the third centile – that gave us a great sense of satisfaction and confidence; it was one of the first things we did that was a departure from the advice given by the medics, who were well meaning, but who didn't know William, in the way that we, as his parents, were getting to know him.

Because William was so physically dependent, we had a lot of physical contact with him. He needed dressing, undressing, lifting into his buggy, putting into his chair and standing frame, bathing and washing, feeding, propping up for a drink, lifting in and out of the car, lifting into bed, and carrying up and down stairs; his teeth needed to be cleaned and his nappies had to be changed. This level of dependency and the close physical contact definitely helped us to develop bonds with William in a way that might have been more difficult if he'd been more independent. If he had been able to feed himself, run off in a tantrum, use the toilet without help, and so on, my guess is that it would have taken much longer to get as close to him as we now have.

For the first year after William came to live with us, Evie took adoption leave so that she could be around for William and the other children as much as possible. When he moved in with us it was agreed that he should continue attending the special nursery he'd been used to in Edinburgh for three days a week. This would give him some continuity of routine and therapy – he had physiotherapy and speech therapy at the nursery – and make the transition a bit easier for him. After the summer, we also enrolled him in the local mainstream nursery for two days a week, so that he could begin getting to know the local children. There was a problem getting the finance agreed, for transport to and from Edinburgh, and it took several weeks for it to be sorted out. In the meantime, Evie had to make two round trips to Edinburgh daily. This meant about four hours travelling time in total, and it was another real burden we could have done without. After we had formally complained, authorisation was at last given for a taxi, and life immediately became much easier. I was struck at how remote from the reality of adoption senior managers can become. I still get angry when I think about it – it was such an unnecessary pressure to put us under.

We continued to have regular co-ordination meetings after William moved in with us. The purpose of these was to see to practical matters, ensure all the therapeutic arrangements were in hand, and to look at contact issues. These meetings were generally attended by William's social worker and her senior, our social worker, and, at first, his previous foster carer, Janet. Looking back at the minutes of the meetings I am struck at how positive they seemed to be, which isn't my memory of that time. I think, despite the difficulties, Evie and I were determined to give it our best shot and didn't allow ourselves to think openly about giving up. No one at the co-ordination meetings mentioned the option of backing out. It wasn't on the agenda. They had all invested a lot in William's placement with us, and the stakes for everyone were very high, and the consequences for William very bleak if it did not work out.

There were of course some good times in those early weeks. William has always had a cheeky, engaging, humorous personality, and can astonish us even now with some of the things he comes out with: the other night as I was tucking him up in bed he said that it was sad, wasn't it, that it was Gordon Brown's last budget! He listens carefully to everything that's going on, has an amazing memory and has his own take on the world. He can have surprising wisdom and insight: 'I don't know why I lose my temper the way I do, Daddy. Sometimes I just have all these angry feelings inside me and they don't know where to go.' Back in the early days, these endearing characteristics helped that mysterious bonding process to begin, so that compassion did eventually metamorphose into love.

William was a full-time job for one or both of us from the outset. He woke early and had to have breakfast before his taxi arrived on nursery days. We tried to get him into bed by seven thirty, and a spin off of this was that we had some time for the other children. They were all physically independent by that stage, but there was always homework, and what we jokingly referred to as "Quality Time". We still do. 'Anyone fancy a walk? A bit of QT?' They rarely take me up on it these days, probably assuming I have a need to talk about the dangers of alcohol, drugs, careers or whatever. 'Sorry, Dad, I'm going out.' 'Sorry, Dad, I've got to, er, tidy my room.' A likely story. The older ones had been used to doing things as a family, and we worried that they would miss this, now that the activities had to be geared to William's needs. Maybe they did, but it wasn't obvious at the time.

Robbie was the biggest worry because he was the youngest and shared a room with William. We persevered with this arrangement for a time, but it became clear that

Robbie needed his space. William also tended to wake at night and disturb Robbie, so we decided to sacrifice our little study and convert it to a very small bedroom for William. He was upset at being moved – he always resists any sort of change – but he eventually made the transition and things became a bit easier. Later we had a downstairs extension built so that William could have his own room and en-suite shower room.

Over the years William has taken over more and more of the house. It's just as well that Evie and I have never been particularly materialistic. Even so, when he first moved in, with his little standing frame and his special chair, and his vast collection of toys, our already disordered house was thrown into chaos, and that has increased over the years. We now have an enormous standing frame, a special bed, two wheelchairs, a shower chair on wheels, a special table, two special chairs, more and more toys (none of which he will allow us to hand on), not to mention his budgie! None of this is particularly aesthetically pleasing, and at first I was conscious of it. If there's an opposite to Feng Shui, our house is a manifestation of it! Now I just don't notice any more, and certainly don't care. I think that's maybe symbolic of the gradual, unconditional absorption of William into our lives.

Those first weeks and months were also a time when William had to be introduced into our wider family and circle of friends. We had a memorable trip to my parents in Cumbria, getting stuck in the snow on the way back, and also visited Evie's parents in Yorkshire. They were all very welcoming. William was at his most engaging and charming, and, like the other children, called them grandma and granddad and granny and grampa respectively, from the start. My dad wanted to know about whether or when he would walk. I think he was a bit alarmed about how we'd manage as William grew up. We were a bit vague in our answer to that one.

Our friends were also welcoming of William, though some were wary of interacting with him and of offering any help. Many of our friends' children had not had contact with disabled children before, and visibly recoiled at the way William thrashed about when he had a muscle spasm. They also asked us, not William, questions about him, as they assumed he wouldn't understand them. It was a learning curve for everyone, and still is; we have to educate all the new folk who keep coming into our lives.

Once William was with us it was too late for our friends to openly tell us how crackers they thought we were, so they presumably confined such discussion to themselves. 'What on earth can have got into Evie and Robert? Why couldn't they just enjoy life? Why couldn't they be content with what they've got? What about their children? What will happen when they get old? Do you think he'll ever walk? What on earth are they trying to prove?' I think some were just not able to contemplate looking after such a needy, fragile looking child. And it was (is) hard work. Evie and I have never been great socialites, but for the first few months we didn't go out together at all. William couldn't be left on his own during the day for more than a few minutes. In fact, thinking about it, that is pretty much the case now, except it has just become such a part of our lives that we aren't conscious of it any more.

I honestly can't remember when I began to really love William. For the first two years at least it was a case of working hard and investing time and attention in him, but I think it was largely done out of a sense of duty. For Evie, love came sooner; she threw herself into that role of "irrational advocate", and pursued his needs like a lioness. But for me it was a slow business. The initial panic subsided, and after a few weeks I knew we were committed and that we'd persevere. I stopped thinking, 'What have we done?' And I stopped working out how long it would be before he reached the age of eighteen and we could re-gain our freedom! But the love came, slowly. When Evie and William went away for the weekend, I found that I really missed him. I became protective of him at parents' evenings at the nursery. I was proud of his efforts to swim, and I was flattered when he shouted, 'come and look at this daddy,' in the museum. So gradually, the boy we adopted became our son, and slowly, we earned the right to be his parents.

William has more official birthdays than the Queen. There's his actual birthday, celebrated with a little party, complete with a cake topped by flickering candles, followed by rowdy games with his friends. Evie and I usually get a bit pensive afterwards, when we think about the circumstances surrounding his birth. Then there's his moving in day, when he first came to live with us, which we celebrate with a special family meal. The seemingly most important date is the anniversary of the day the adoption order was granted. But we don't really celebrate it, maybe because it was such an anti-climax at the time. We'd all made the trip to court, about twenty miles away, having dressed up especially for the occasion. Our big moment was sandwiched between criminal cases, one of which involved violent offences, and had lots of whispering, chain-smoking witnesses outside, with tattooed knuckles, unshaven chins and the odd facial scar. Eventually we were shown in to see the sheriff in his chambers. Reports written by our social worker and a curator *ad litem* (an officer appointed by the court) were strewn across his desk. 'Well, that all seems to be in order,' he said, rather officiously, and he signed the papers with more of a grin than a smile. We didn't find the courage to ask him to pose with William for a photo, but we did take one on the court steps afterwards.

5

Cast of a thousand

If you're not careful, when you adopt a child with disabilities your circle of acquaintances becomes much wider and the number of friends you have slowly falls! Your life gets taken over by the care of your child and with appointments with a host of professionals. You have less time for socialising, and it's hard to get a baby-sitter.

Reviews, co-ordination meetings, planning meetings, appointments with various specialists and therapists. Meetings, meetings, meetings. Sometimes William can have three appointments a week with different people, and at other times we can go for several weeks without any. Some appointments involve just one therapist – an occupational therapist, a teacher or a doctor, and at other times the professionals fill the room. We have a friend who described a review that took place in her house, because of the nature of her child's disability it made this the easiest place. Participants kept on arriving and she shuttled more and more mugs of tea and coffee through from the kitchen. The doorbell went again and she told the man on the step to go through and asked him if he'd like tea or coffee. He declined both and she warmed to him immediately. He had an odd looking machine under his arm; another therapeutic device, she thought. When she joined the meeting he was standing in the middle of the room, looking a bit perplexed, surrounded by a host of smiling, seated men and women, sipping their coffee and tucking in to her chocolate chip cookies. 'I've just come to read your electric meter,' he said, holding up his machine.

We made a list once, of the various people involved in William's care, education and health. He was going to two schools at the time – a special one with small classes of half a dozen children, and lots of therapy on site, and the local mainstream primary school, with a full-time teaching assistant and visiting therapists. So the list comprised: two teachers, three classroom assistants, an occupational therapist (health), another occupational therapist (local authority), a speech and language therapist (mainly for eating difficulties), a physiotherapist, one social worker from the adoption agency, another from the local authority, the community paediatrician, consultant neurologist and orthopaedic surgeon, our health visitor and general practitioner, staff from "Brainwave", a voluntary organisation supporting families and their brain damaged children and an instructor from Riding for the Disabled, a teacher for the visually impaired, an eye consultant, the home care organiser and some managers. The list came to about thirty.

William knows all of them by name, and understands their different roles. He revels in attention and generally speaking interacts well with all of the various folk in his life. He asks sensible questions, such as this one, posed during a visit to the neurologist:

'Dr Erikson, can you explain to me why I am afraid of car sunroofs?'

Dr Erikson turned to his trainee enquiringly, possibly for inspiration, possibly to test his child-centred bedside manner.

'Maybe it's your depth perception,' the young trainee

suggested after a pause, twiddling his stethoscope, which dangled over his child-friendly Winnie the Pooh tie. 'Maybe it gives things a bit of a scary look?'

'Yes, I've wondered about that,' William concurred with a wise expression. Dr Erikson nodded approvingly.

In fact, we later discovered from his former foster carers that William's fear of car sunroofs probably stems from a time when he was very young and a helium balloon he was holding escaped his grasp and was whipped up through the open car sunroof and into the stratosphere. He was distraught at the loss, and there's probably some subconscious association. It's fascinating how a brief, seemingly inconsequential incident, which took place before William had learned to speak, could have had such a profound impact upon him. William still sometimes gets distressed when he goes in the car, screaming in terror at the sunroof. It's hard to imagine the emotional impact of all the other traumas and losses he's experienced. And even though we now think we know the cause of his fear of sunroofs, it's very difficult to help William overcome it. It makes you realise the challenge involved in helping children overcome profoundly troubling experiences.

William is less co-operative with other therapists. Our long-suffering OT (occupational therapist) has been trying for months to get a sleep system in place that will keep William's legs in position. The most comfortable sleeping position for him is to sleep on his back, but the progressive nature of his CP (cerebral palsy) means his legs twist to the side. This could lead to hip and spine misalignment or hip dislocation so we need to find a way of keeping his legs and pelvis aligned while he is sleeping. 'Oh no, not again,' he groans when we announce that the OT will be round later with another contraption. Then it's an hour of pulling him around and trying various bits of equipment, which he generally finds uncomfortable and restricting.

Some of the appointments have little tangible benefit

for him or for us. A letter comes: 'Please report to so and so on such and such a date so that we can review William's progress.' It's a case of arranging time off work and keeping William off school, then sometimes a long car journey, for what feels like a bit of superfluous form ticking, followed by, 'Well, that's all fine then. I'd like to see William in another six months.' Not that monitoring is not important, as long as the purpose is clear and the various appointments are co-ordinated, if possible, or – how's this for a radical suggestion – combined!

Without exception all of William's therapists are very helpful and approachable, and we have good relationships with them. It wasn't so easy at the beginning. Some seemed suspicious of us, and of course we were beginners in understanding and managing disability issues. I remember looks of pity when we asked what the likelihood was of William being able to walk. In the first couple of years we had to adjust to this most difficult aspect of his disabilities. We had been given to understand that he would be likely to walk with an aid, and we have a video of him doing just that before he was placed with us. In fact the videos of his early life are a bit depressing to look at now: despite all our efforts, his disability now looks much more pronounced. The "developing" nature of his CP means that he is very unlikely to walk. This was explained to us by the neurologist after William came to live with us. As he grows older his muscles tighten, and his legs become less and less able to bear his weight. He cannot stand unaided, or hold himself up. His fine motor skills are very poor, he has a visual impairment, feeding difficulties, suffers from agonising migraines, which lead to bouts of severe vomiting about once a fortnight, doesn't like food much and needs help with just about everything. Our approach is to try to maximise the potential he has in the face of the relentless advance of the effects of CP as he grows.

The larger gatherings of "the professionals" were

particularly stressful in the early days, and sometimes still are. There was a tension between the professionals and us. You could almost see them expecting to have problems in their dealings with us. Many parents of children with disabilities are angry. Their children have complex needs. Life is just about manageable when everyone involved sticks to the arrangements, but it can become very difficult when they don't: 'They've forgotten to send his rain cape home – what will we do in the morning if it rains?' 'Look, he's hardly eaten any of his packed lunch – and I told them that he needs to be encouraged. No wonder he's got a headache.' Other parents complain that the school taxi arrives late, or too early or there's a last minute change of escort and Susie refuses to get in the car because things are different. So parents become angry, professionals become apprehensive of making contact, the parents pick this up and become angrier still. Day-to-day life in the world of disability can be very complicated. And then there are the big decisions: mainstream or special school; whether to elect for surgery or not; whether to adapt the house; whether to accept the offer of respite.

It can be very difficult picking your way through the maze of services. There's an OT in health who deals with sleep systems and special chairs; there's an OT in the local authority who deals with adaptations; there's another OT who deals with general assessment and aids to daily living. The physio deals with the standing frame, and the wheelchair comes from a hospital, but the community health OT seems to be the co-ordinator. It can all be very confusing.

William spends a lot of time in his wheelchair. When he first moved from a buggy to a wheelchair a few years back, they were all set to give him one with small wheels that he would be unable to push himself. Eventually they agreed he could try out a self-propelling one, and he quickly took to wheeling himself around, albeit a bit slowly. So we were given a self-propelling chair. As he's grown, so we've had to upgrade from time to time. Earlier this year it was agreed that he needed a lighter, more manoeuvrable wheelchair. We wanted the best available in order to maximise his independence. The health authority was only prepared to give William the best their supplier can provide. There are lighter, more manoeuvrable wheelchairs on the market, and we asked if instead of providing the standard chair, they could give us the funds and we'd top up to get the more superior one. But of course, for some tangled bureaucratic reason this was not possible. After a six month wait the chair finally arrived. In the meantime, William has had a growth spurt so it only just fits! It is not "crash-tested" to a high standard, and does not come with a headrest, so he can't use it safely in vehicles. We'll probably end up with two wheelchairs – the one supplied by the NHS and one bought privately.

There are so many issues you could do battle over – it's not surprising that some parents get angry. But many parents just haven't the energy to keep on fighting. Proportionally more disabled children are brought up by lone parents than other children, presumably because of the strain the care task places on relationships. There is also a link between poverty and disabled children, so, given the work involved in caring for a child with disabilities, it's not surprising that many parents are worn out. We're incredibly lucky with all the supports we have.

We have been invited several times to take part in focus groups and service planning groups – Evie tends to be the one to go – and often there is only a handful of parents. The rest are too tired or disaffected, or can't face the emotional agony. And often the results bear little relation to the reality experienced by most parents and children; fine glossy publications that impress social services inspectors but make little real difference to day-to-day life.

The network of contacts isn't confined to the statutory

agencies. Some years ago we heard about "Brainwave" – a voluntary organisation in Somerset, which devises programmes of "do it yourself" physiotherapy for parents to carry out with children who have brain injuries. We took William down and spent a couple of days being assessed and trained in the techniques, and we have been in contact ever since. It was a round trip of about seven hundred miles to their centre in Bridgewater. In later years we began combining the trips with camping holidays in the south, towing a trailer with all the necessary gear, and more recently Brainwave has been offering reassessments in Scotland. We sometimes meet other families during our visits to Brainwave. It is very humbling to have glimpses into the lives of families who have children with really severe and life-shortening conditions. The love and dedication of the parents is amazing. Our life is a doddle by comparison.

Then there are organisations like Riding for the Disabled. Being perched on a wobbling horse has certainly helped William develop strength in his trunk. The organisers all take it very seriously and professionally and do a wonderful job. The recent highlight of the local association was when Princess Anne flew in by helicopter to watch a display and to give out rosettes. William was very put out that she didn't answer his question: 'What's it like being a princess?' 'That's what comes of mumbling, William,' we told him afterwards. We were introduced to the princess as 'marvellous people who adopted that lovely little ginger-haired boy'. And we both looked around for a stone to crawl under.

In some ways we feel on the fringe of the "disability world", and on the whole are happy with that. It may sound strange, but sometimes it's easy for us to forget that William is disabled, though less so now that he is getting bigger, and the differences between him and his peers are more pronounced. At first, our pattern of activities and holidays hardly changed. We went camping and travelled to Spain and France. We have a Canadian canoe with a special seat in it for William, and we still go youth hostelling. His wheelchair has been hauled over terrain that would defy the most rugged four by four. I remember one holiday on the wild, west coast of Scotland when the six of us were negotiating a tricky path strewn with boulders and bog. We had found a sheep tick in William's navel the day before and he'd become wary of exposing himself to go to the loo outside, so we'd collectively made up a humorous song to try and neutralise his fear:

> *Don't expose your buttocks to the sheep ticks*
> *Sheep ticks*
> *Or the sheep ticks they will sink their teeth in you*
> *But with a clever arrangement of mirrors*
> *You can see them hanging on*
> *When you go off to the loo to do a poo*
> *Poo, Poo poo.*
> *Don't expose etc.*

On the third refrain, as we rounded a grassy mound, we stumbled upon a pair of very refined elderly water colourists, who, in the face of our vulgarity, managed to retain their dignity by entirely ignoring us and our song, cut prematurely short, but picked up again when they were out of hearing range.

'Just act normal, family.'

We are sometimes asked if having a disabled *child* means that we look upon ourselves as a *disabled family*; in other words whether we are *all* restricted in the things we do because of William's needs. To a degree it is inevitable that William curtails our freedom, but on the other hand, since he joined the family we have always tried to carry on as normal. Having children is a life-choice with consequences for the whole family, whatever the needs of the child. William poses certain restrictions on what we can do, but so do the others: teenagers who no longer want to go on holiday with us and who can't understand why we won't agree to leave them at home on their own; harp-playing offspring who need to be driven to performances the length and breadth of the country, and so on. We've never felt particularly restricted as a result of William's disability. Maybe because we adopted him knowing of his disability, and expecting a change in lifestyle, it was easier for us to adjust than it might be for a birth family unprepared to parent a disabled child.

William goes to the local Catholic school around the corner from where we live. There are a few other disabled pupils in the school. Sometimes their parents gather at the gates in the morning after dropping off the children. I always give them a cheery good morning as I go past, but don't tend to linger. On the whole we tend to try and sort out concerns and problems by ourselves. It can be hard to find like-minded people in a small community. Occasionally we group together with other parents to look at issues such as access or inclusion.

We know a few parents of disabled children who are aware that William is adopted, but we don't really know what they think of us. Right at the beginning a friend who has a disabled daughter expressed incredulity that we were adopting a child with disabilities, though it's very plain how much she loves her own daughter. Then she added, 'but at least you won't have the guilt,' and she went on to explain the irrational guilt that hatched when her child was born – the feeling that it was all somehow her fault, and the gnawing regret that is impossible to shake off and that stays with parents forever. No, we don't have that kind of guilt, but we feel guilty because we never feel we do enough to maximise William's potential. Who knows, with more physio and time, he might be more independent than he is. It's much easier and quicker to lift him from his wheelchair and sit him on the loo than it is to use a transfer board and encourage him to slide from his wheelchair to his commode chair and back again. There are many more situations that can evoke the "if only we had" guilt-laden feeling.

We have a couple of acquaintances who each have children with CP and who have each devised daily programmes of physio lasting several hours a day, which involve teams of helpers and volunteers. One of the children (now an adult) has made spectacular progress, and the other is still severely disabled, with no speech or independent movement. We know another family who elected not to have physiotherapy at all, because their son hated it so much and it left no time for anything else. One of the most difficult aspects of parenting a child with disabilities is that this sort of decision can impact on the child forever. And, yes, there's always the guilt that you have done the wrong thing or may not have done enough.

We had a difficult decision to make a couple of years back, when we were asked to consider whether William should have a pump installed internally to deliver a drug to his spine to prevent tightening of his muscles. It meant opting for non-essential invasive surgery which would result in a device the size and weight of a round glass ashtray being inserted under his skin in the abdomen area, with tubes leading to his spine. In the end we went for it, and William spent about ten days in hospital, with one of us on a camp-bed nearby, followed by a further three weeks at home recovering. He was nauseous for days and his tummy became alarmingly distended. 'Try tight clothing,' said the consultant, and we purloined an elastic, silver, sequin-covered crop top from the daughter of a neighbour. William was persuaded to look upon it as chain mail. Eventually the swelling went down as the fluid was reabsorbed. We still feel a bit mixed about the surgery. On the positive side, his hamstrings are not as tight as they were, but on the other hand, he has less strength in his legs (the tightening of the hamstrings was a false strength, but it did nevertheless enable him to stand with support). And he drools more, which is possibly a side-effect. I think the reality is that parents feel guilty whatever they do; there's no right or wrong way, and there's lots of uncertainty. It's a great boost when people say, 'Oh, isn't William coming on well,' even when you're not sure they really mean it!

It's not easy to work out what his disability means to William himself. My mother is now quite frail and walks with an aid. When he asked her why she needed a walker a couple of years back she explained that her legs were not working properly: 'A bit like yours William.' He looked at her, with surprise. 'There's nothing wrong with my legs, Grandma,' he said. Sometimes he seems to deny his disability, or be unaware of it. It's all he's known, so I suppose for him it's his yardstick for normality. And that's quite a good attitude, and might boost his self-esteem. At times, though, the denial is painful. He goes to the after school football club, and basically sits in front of goals while the other children play around him. His visual impairment means he can't see the ball too well, and he can't move quickly enough and he isn't strong enough to prevent a goal. So unless the ball happens to strike his chair he doesn't contribute much to the game. He insists on going though – probably for the social contact – and while it's all a bit uncomfortable for us as parents to watch, we feel he needs to take part if he wants to, and work it all out in his own way. But it takes us about an hour to get his feet warmed up again when we get home. William has very poor circulation in his legs, and his feet turn to blocks of ice on even slightly chilly days, despite being cocooned in mohair socks. Then it takes another half an hour to wash the mud off the wheels!

Recently, we've begun to question more seriously the value of William participating in football. Now that the children in William's class are getting a bit older and bigger, the pace of the game has picked up, and for

William's own safety, the supervising teacher has moved him to the side of the goalmouth. There's another child with disabilities in the team, and he and William job-share the role of goalkeeper. But what message does this arrangement give them and the other children? At best it is a statement that disabled children sometimes need to be looked after by the others, but at worst it implies that they can't really take part; that in effect William's contribution to the game is useless; that his presence is tolerated rather than valued. There is a danger that this perception by the other children on the football field affects how he is viewed off the pitch too. It's a very difficult dilemma for us as parents: it's great that the school includes William in the way they do – after all, this is a voluntary, extra curricular activity – but in some ways it actually reinforces the exclusion of children with disabilities. We're planning to talk to the school about alternative sports that William could participate in more equally; in the meantime, like the others in his class, he wants to go along to football after school!

But William can also be quite wily about his disability: 'I can't do my homework tonight. I am disabled you know.' More recently he seems to have had some flashes of insight: 'I hate being a wheelchair user.'

We sometimes talk with William about the need for him to try and become more independent, so that he can do more for himself, but it is hard work getting him to understand why this is important. 'You're getting so big and good at transferring, and Mum and I have sore backs, so it would be good if we didn't have to lift you so much' and 'Now that you are ten years old you need to eat your dinner by yourself' and 'Why don't you try pushing your wheelchair to the end of the road instead of me pushing it?...' He shows little inclination to be independent, and is hard to motivate, despite our best creative efforts. Ed recently drew a chart with a picture of William at one end of a path leading to a cinema, with ten steps in between. William ticked a step on the chart each time he ate a meal without help. It took him about three weeks to get to the end, but at last the big day came for him to see *The Simpsons: The Movie*. We couldn't find a newspaper with the cinema times in, but I assured Evie that there would be showings every half hour or so at the Multiplex in town. She should know by now not to listen to me; we managed to miss the last showing and to compensate had to spend ages meandering along the aisles of Toys R Us, next to the cinema. It was William's idea of heaven, and he quivered with excitement when we eventually found the depleted stock of Star Wars toys, and he spent a blissful forty minutes trying to make his mind up about which ones to buy. We've just started another chart ending in a trip to the cinema, but of course William now knows that the destination is much more of a mystery tour. It will be interesting to see how it affects his motivation...

When William gets up in the morning, one of his little jobs is to lower his electric bed, so the mattress does not get a permanent bend in it. All that is involved is pressing a switch and holding it down for a few seconds. But every morning, he objects: 'Why do I have to do this? Why can't you do it? How come I'm expected to do everything around here!?' We suspect his reluctance stems from a mixture of the real physical effort that is required for him to perform even simple tasks, and an emotional need to be cared for, arising from his disrupted early years. As he grows older and bigger, our efforts to get him to become more independent are increasing!

William has only once ever alluded to his disability as a reason he was unable to stay with his birth mother: 'Was my tummy mummy not able to look after me because she was ill and I needed lots of care because of my disability...?'

Despite William's apparent lack of insight about his

disability for much of the time, he shows touching compassion for others with disabilities, particularly adults. We recently visited my aunt, who is now severely disabled with Parkinson's. William sat beside her bed, holding her hand, and chatting away easily to her. Periodically he'd call out: 'Be quiet everybody, Aunty Mary is trying to say something!' When we were on holiday we met a man with multiple sclerosis with whom William quickly struck up a friendship: 'So, Bill, is your house all on one level? Do you have someone who comes in to help you? How do you manage on the bus…?'

Curiously, William seems less easy with other disabled children. During a recent hydrotherapy session he was asking the mothers of the other children about the sort of things they liked doing: 'Does Fergus like swimming? Does he like Star Wars?' He is a ten-year-old boy with all the usual insensitivity of that age.

'Why don't you ask Fergus yourself?' suggested Evie. We always have to bite our lip when other people and children put questions to us rather than directly to William.

We wonder if William might have achieved more of his obvious potential if he hadn't been adopted, and I think the answer is undoubtedly "yes", if he'd had the right care and security from his birth family. It can be very difficult to get him to do anything physical, whether it is eating, crawling, propelling his wheelchair or trying to write. These tasks are all hard work for him. I think trying to write his name must be a bit like me trying to write my name using a pen held between the toes of my left foot. But as well as the physical challenges, the emotional upheaval of his early life, and the consequent lack of early attachments, his sense of insecurity and his low self-esteem, must all be significant in terms of his motivation. He loves the attention that comes with being helped with physical tasks, and he still has a strong emotional need for physical closeness. Although this has helped us to bond with him, it may have slowed the rate at which he is acquiring self-help skills. It's also a very frustrating facet of his character. You know that if you ask him to do something involving effort, like putting his toys back in their box, he'll moan, complain and whine and take ages, not just because it is hard work for him, but because he doesn't want to do it, like most children of course. When you're trying to cook the dinner, are tired after a long day at work, need to get the washing in off the line because it's started to rain, have to answer the phone, have just tripped over the demented dog, can't find the vegetable peeler, can't hear yourself think because Robbie is having a band practice upstairs and so on, it's hard sometimes not to snap. 'Come on William; it's not a big job,' and then in rising pitch, 'Just put the ones you can reach in the box, can't you see how much I've got to do?' Finally, after more moaning from William: 'Okay, if you don't help me with this one thing there's no more TV tonight.' Or something like that. It's hard being a rational adult all of the time or even most of the time. I often end up apologising to William and the others afterwards: 'I'm sorry I lost my cool, but there's so much to do...' and they smile and humour me till next time. But in some ways it's good that William sees that we lose our temper and get stressed. At the risk of finding an excuse, you could say it helps him learn about relationships and social interaction.

William occasionally asks why he is disabled, and we explain that nobody knows really, but that he was born early and didn't start breathing quickly enough. It's very difficult to give him full details about his parents' misuse of drugs and lifestyle. He has a life story book he turns to periodically with basic information, and that's enough for him for now. He did ask recently if he loses his temper the way he does, because his birth parents used to have arguments together (this is explained in the life story book), and we reassured him that there was no link; we all lose our tempers at times, and we all become our own people as we grow older.

Sometimes it can feel that William is being entirely unreasonable, and we are left wondering whether it is an aspect of his disability or whether it is associated with his early life experiences and attachment difficulties. The other day, at his request, we met up with his former foster carer after a gap of about three years. We'd chosen the neutral ground of a café in a shopping centre. He asked her lots of questions about the time he spent with her and the meeting seemed to go fairly well. He was understandably tearful when he said goodbye. We had arranged that he would spend that night with his godparents, whom he is very fond of. We had anticipated that he might be upset and thought this visit would help him get over it. And we had the exciting prospect of a night off. A foolish error of judgement on our part! We spoke to them and him on the phone later, and he was distinctly wobbly. 'Would you like to come home William?' 'I think so. I don't know. Come and get me.' When we got there he just didn't know what he wanted, so we took charge and told him we'd take him home. He immediately erupted into a spectacular tantrum, the pitch and extent of which is impossible to adequately describe. He was incandescent with rage and it lasted for two hours, as we loaded him and all his things into the car and drove home. We felt we had to follow our decision through, particularly as he'd hinted that he had a migraine coming on, and we didn't want the poor godparents to have to deal with that. He was wholly irrational.

'Why do I have to go home?'

'Because you said you wanted to, William.'

'Well, I was lying! I hate you. First you take me from my foster mum, then you take me from my godparents...' And so on, no matter how carefully and patiently we explained the reasons. Is it just the disappointed reaction any child would have? Our other children never behaved quite so extremely in the face of disappointment. Is it to do with attachment issues? Is it to do with cognitive difficulties? Answers on a postcard please. Along with advice about how we might have handled it all better! In reality it's probably a mixture of all of these things. William has a lot to be angry about.

Once home the migraine developed and he was very sick. The next day he was the personification of sweetness and charm; a child you couldn't help but love, in contrast to the monster of the previous day. It's a bit of a pattern; it's almost as if he has to go through these crises from time to time to get them out of his system. Evie and I have to tell each other: 'Don't take it personally.'

So, whilst there is a cast of a thousand, no one really has the answers to what you should do. You develop your own expertise, with help along the way of course, and in the light of experience, mistakes, sleepless nights, trial and error. But at the end of the day it is the parents who are the experts, more so than all the consultants and teachers and therapists and theorists put together. All children are different and you have to live with them to get remotely close to what makes them tick and what works. There's a lot of talk in professional circles about the notion of parents as partners in planning and delivering services. There is some way to go before their expertise is as valued as it should be.

6

The adoption triangle

My eighty-six year old father is piecing together our family tree at the moment. He is the oldest of nine children who survived beyond infancy, though only four are still living. His mother was one of eight; it was the norm in those days. The tree is more like a sprawling bush, with very complicated ganglions of tendrils, shoots and roots, all of which are nonetheless bound together, though farther back other seeds from the bush have got blown to new ground and become lost. There are a few dark places in the shade and beneath the soil: whispered rumours of a child born out of wedlock here, in the 1940s, and in the 1920s a spell of imprisonment for my great grandfather for horse stealing. Romantic stuff for us, looking back, but probably nightmarish for everyone at the time. And grinding rural poverty that you can see in the faces of the crumpled photos that dad pores over as he assembles his family's life into a chart that summarises the diverse, sprawling blood-connections. There's a craze for family trees at the moment: CD-ROMs which show you how to trace your ancestors come free with the Sunday supplements, and emotional celebrities trace their humble roots on TV for the entertainment of the public. It was a revelation to see Jeremy Paxman cry!

William arrived in our family with a diagram of his own family tree – a page in his "life story book", partly completed and neatly arranged in a yellow ring binder. He always chooses yellow if he's given a choice: his room is painted yellow, his favourite T-shirts are yellow, and our next car has to be yellow. The family tree only goes as far back as his grandparents, still in their prime. His social worker has put photos of his mother and some of his siblings in plastic inserts, with captions underneath saying who is who, with a narrative of events phrased in a way that cushions some of the grim reality. There are no photos of his birth dad, his youngest brother, his grandparents or other family members. There are pictures of William with the various foster carers who looked after him during the first year of his life, and many more of Janet. The album sits on one of the bookshelves in his room, next to another, smaller album of us: of his new family that we had put together in preparation for his move. The albums are separate. The families are separate, with only William connecting the two. He can just about hold an album in each hand at the same time.

William has an impressive grasp of who's who in the Marsden clan, and in Evie's extended family, both of which are very sizeable. He sees some of them only once a year, but has made a real connection with them, asking Grandad how aunty Mary is after her recent illness, and getting sad at the death of Evie's cousin, whom he'd never met. Signs, maybe, of a growing sense of belonging and place. At the same time it must be hard for him to make sense of where he fits in to this complicated tangle of family networks.

William had an exercise to do for homework the other day. It is one of the features of going to a Catholic school – little exercises to connect the children with the family of God. Not that that is in itself a bad thing; so far school has been a very positive experience for William, and the affirming, caring ethos has been exactly what he needs. It's just that sometimes, even now, in our multi-cultural country where the popularly understood meaning of "family" has become diverse and rich, sweeping assumptions are made about children's histories and experiences. There were various questions he had to answer for this exercise:

> *Where have we come from?*
> *Mark in the main days of your life so far – for example, I learned to walk; I was baptised; I started school; I began to write; I began to talk; I was born; my first communion, etc…*

It's easy to be over-sensitive and get worked up too quickly. We knew what lay ahead when we embarked on this particular exercise. We muttered and banged the pots about in the kitchen, while William watched TV in the living room. We were cross about the insensitivity of it all, but we also tried to treat it with a bit of wry humour. The truth for William would read something like this:

> *I was born ten weeks premature because my mother used drugs and did not look after herself.*
> *I was addicted to heroin at birth and it had to be withdrawn slowly.*
> *I was on a life support machine for a while because my brain was starved of oxygen when I was born. I spent the first three months of my life in hospital. I was diagnosed as having cerebral palsy and microcephalus. My mum didn't come to see me much.*
> *Then I went home for a few days but my mum couldn't manage and I went to stay with foster carers.*
> *After going home again for a few days I went to various other foster carers and it was decided that I should be adopted.*
> *After a while I went to live with my new family. I really missed my last foster carers, who I had been with for*

three years.

Most of the time I love my new family, but I still wonder about my other family, and don't fully understand why they couldn't look after me.

My tummy mummy wanted me to be brought up as a Catholic. I was baptised at the cathedral; the local priest wasn't keen to baptise me in his church because my adoptive parents aren't Catholic.

I started two schools when I was five – the local one and another one about twenty miles away for children with disabilities.

I can't walk but I can use a wheelchair.

I can't write, because my fine motor skills are poor, and I've got a visual impairment, but I'm learning to type.

I haven't had my first communion yet – it's a bit of a problem that my mum and dad aren't Catholics...

And so on.

We do, of course, alert William's teacher to the issues apparently innocuous exercises like this one can raise, but if you're not careful you'd be forever fighting battles, and you need to choose the ones you can win and the ones you've got the energy for. And of course William needs to be able to deal with the reality of who he is, even if it is a bit complicated for a child with his background. All the time new people we meet ask us: 'Where does he get his ginger hair from?' and 'What was he like as a baby?' In fact, he's probably better at dealing with these questions than we are, and often when he's meeting people for the first time he'll tell them with disarming ease that he's adopted, and launch into a detailed description of who's who in his life. Evie once dyed her hair red at William's request, as a mark of solidarity, but looked as if she was wearing a ginger cat on her head, so she reverted to type fairly quickly. William was convulsed with giggles, but also touched at the effort.

So after we'd calmed down and had our tea, we sat round the table – Mum, Dad and William – and came up with this for the school exercise:

> *I was born on 23 April 1997.*
>
> *I lived with my foster carer, Auntie Janet and Uncle John from 1998 to 2001.*
>
> *I went to live with my new family in January 2001.*
>
> *I was adopted in August 2001.*
>
> *I was baptised in June 2002 and have three godmothers and a godfather.*
>
> *I am in touch with two of my birth brothers.*
>
> *I started at St. Chrispin's school on...*

We helped William to fill in the chart, and he coloured in some of the pictures, which was a real struggle for him because of his poorly developed fine motor skills. And colouring in is pretty boring at the best of times. Then he wanted to look through his life story book; something he hadn't done since Evie's uncle visited from Canada a few months before – that too triggered questions and a need to try and work things out again. He turned the pages quietly for a while, looking at the images of his other family. He knows each picture and each trapped expression so well. A smiling image means a happy person, and he's got a distorted view of how things were. There are no pictures of the family rows, the drug-taking, the children left crying in their cots – and how things probably are now, though we know very little of his birth family's current situation. Then it was time for his shower and bed.

'I don't want to go to bed. Why do I have to go to bed? I don't like you any more. I never wanted to be a part of this family,' getting more and more unreasonable, holding the rims of his wheelchair so it was impossible to push. And all this, of course, after a long day at work when we're tired and when it's difficult to deal with things in the way you know you should. And all the old questions like 'Why can't I live with my tummy mummy?' and 'Why did you adopt me anyway?' After six years! So bedtime was a bit late while we took time to put questions back to him – 'What do you think, William?' – and tried to reinforce our place as parents. 'We chose you out of all the other children who were looking for a new family.' And we told him we loved him and were so pleased that he was in our family. And eventually we got him showered and into bed and we had our little bedtime routine with two glove puppets chatting to him, followed by a story. Then a kiss and he said, ' I love you, Mum and Dad'. And the album got put back on the shelf, till the next time.

Later, when the washing up was done and Robbie had finally been persuaded to do his homework, Evie and I debriefed over a glass of wine, with a little background music. We're used to these chain reactions: something occurs which sparks off a series of questions in his head, and puts him in touch with feelings, deep inside. And the questions are just about impossible to answer, not only because of the limited information we have but because at their core they are about self-esteem and worth. How can William make sense of the fact that some of his brothers are still with his birth parents and he is not, even when we do all we can to compensate?

He called us back to his room a couple of times. First he'd forgotten to have his glass of water, then he'd dropped one of his countless cuddly toys. He still needs very predictable rituals and routines, especially when he's revisited the past. His room is bursting with toys he no longer plays with, and clothes he's outgrown, but he's not yet ready for us to find new homes for them – he can't let go any of his past – not yet. Sipping our wine we agreed on one thing: we may not share William's blood, but somehow, and at a time we didn't notice, he had become just as wholly our child as the other three.

Dad showed us the latest draft of his family tree on our next visit. Evie and I have our place under him and Mum, and below us are our four children, each linked on dad's chart by the same bold lines. William smiled when Dad showed him. When we got home he asked for the life story book again. We'd got another bottle of wine at the ready!

* * *

The child, the adoptive parents and the birth parents are often described as "the adoption triangle." Each is represented by a point on the triangle, linked together forever by the three lines. It is important that adoptive parents accept that the triangle will always be part of their lives. In the past, not all children were told that they were adopted, or they were told in the middle of adolescence or found out by chance, sometimes with traumatic results. The practice now is for more openness, based on a belief that this leads to better adjustment on the part of the child. It is, however, a challenge for adoptive parents to feel comfortable and confident in managing the complex dynamics, as shown by the family tree incident above. The fallout can be hard work to deal with, although there is little doubt that openness is healthy, even if at times painful. When the worlds of William's birth family and adoptive family collide inside him, he still gets into a rage, the scale of which would astonish our friends if they could see him, because he's normally so very engaging. But at least he feels safe enough to let himself go, and there are signs that his outbursts are becoming less frequent and have slipped in scale from force ten to force nine when they are at their peak.

William is one of six birth children. The information we have about most of the others is frozen in time, in the photographs and captions in his life story book. There are a few photographs of his mother, holding William on her lap during visits to the children's centre, accompanied by her two older children. In one picture she's cradling him in her arms and smiling down at him. They're family snaps, and without the full story could be of any family, caught at random, doing nothing in particular. There's a picture of

William's eldest brother holding him, and of the next one leaning over and grinning. They seem nice boys. At times William longs for them, though he can have no memory of them; he hasn't seen them since he was two. There are three other younger brothers; two have been adopted together and another, the youngest, is still at home, and we don't have any photos of him. They all have the same father, and they all have a similar look about them. The photographs are over six years old and we have no information about what has become of William's birth family since the pictures were taken. We can't answer his questions about them. It's hard for him to picture the older ones as different from the way they appear on the glossy, slippery photos that catch little patches of white electric light as he looks at them. They will be teenagers now: young adults beginning to make their own way somehow. I sometimes wonder how we would all get on if we met. It's an odd feeling to know that your son has brothers out there somewhere, who might or might not be in need, and with whom you have a connection that is difficult to define.

Occasionally William can be preoccupied with his life story book for days on end. It was beginning to feel quite morbid, so we put together an album of his early years in our family, so that he can look back with positive nostalgia and we can share common memories. It seems to have helped.

William's fantasies about his family were strongest when he was younger. He would invent elaborate stories about his relationship with his mother. I remember a winter car journey in safe engulfing darkness, when he talked in minute detail about going swimming with his mother, and how she supported him in the pool and played with him. And how she later took him swimming in the sea and shielded him in the crashing surf. When we asked him whether this was just a story, or something he would have liked to happen, he was adamant that it was all true, and very indignant that we should question it. It's puzzling to know how much to let go and how much to query. Our line was to tell William that he was free to think his own thoughts, though at other times we also helped him piece together the reality of his past – the fact that his mother had only cared for him for a matter of weeks in total.

One aspect of William's birth family that we can keep "real" is his two adopted birth brothers. Marc and Luke were adopted by a childless couple in the west of Scotland before we were matched with William. Marc is literally nine months younger than William and Luke is just under twelve months younger than Marc. We met their adoptive parents, Martin and Margaret, at a Christmas social gathering organised by the adoption society which approved us. They have welcomed William warmly into their wider family. We meet up two or three times a year so the children can have time together.

Margaret and Martin are very generous of spirit and shower William with gifts. They include us in family celebrations, such as birthday parties for the boys and other social gatherings. Interestingly, Marc and Luke never ask their parents about their birth family – maybe being brought up together gives them a stronger sense of identity. They do ask about their relationship with our other three children though, all of whom are attentive towards them and are looked up to as really cool, which is good for William to see, given the hard time he still gives them occasionally. Kate in particular has a special place in the eyes of Marc and Luke, as the nearest thing they have to a sister. They look upon the three of them as their adoptive brothers and sister, or cousins, or something in the middle. It doesn't really seem to matter, as long as we explain the relationships as carefully as we can.

It's great seeing William together with Marc and Luke; there's no doubt they have a strong natural bond of blood, though I suspect William's need to assert the bond is stronger than theirs. It's interesting too, that in spite of the attachment, the signs of sibling rivalry between the three of them come quickly to the fore; within an hour William will be telling tales to get one of the others into trouble, and the children will be to-ing and fro-ing to both sets of parents with complaints about each other. It can be hard to maintain the peace. Evie and I sometimes speculate on how the relationships might have been if the boys had all been placed together – the prospect is almost too exhausting to think about – three children born within two years of each other, all with experiences of grief, loss and change, and one with severe disabilities. The contact they have together is demanding for all the parents but worth it, even if it feels a bit frenetic at the time, as if all the bonding as well as the sibling rivalry have to be concentrated into the brief time they are together.

Martin and Margaret agreed to be William's godparents when he was baptised, and that link has helped to bind him to his wider family, and has strengthened his sense of identity and his self-esteem, though just as our family tree is more like a sprawling bush, our adoption triangle is more of a polygon. We have Marc and Luke to stay over on their own occasionally and William has been to stay with them too. It makes for complicated class discussions at school, when the children are invited to share their news after the weekend. One of William's classmates once accosted me in the playground when I went to collect him at the end of the day, to demand that I refute William's assertion that he'd been to see some mysterious younger brothers the day before. Whilst we are open about William's adoption, there are times when it would be good just to have a bit more privacy. But William has to feel able to share who he is, and he's certainly not bashful about it!

We would have been prepared to have direct contact with other members of William's birth family, but that wasn't being looked for at the time of placement. The possibility of contact in the future and the question as to how he and we might cope with that is something that we have yet to deal with. Evie once thought she recognised William's birth mother in a supermarket checkout queue, from the photographs in William's life story book, and surprised herself at how agitated she became. Of course, when we're in our cosy sitting room together, it's easy to talk rationally about how it's part of the adoptive parents' lot to accept the birth parents for what they are and not to judge, particularly not in front of William. But in the supermarket queue, Evie found herself getting angry with the woman who, from what we know, had caused William's disability through her own irresponsible lifestyle, with no thought for the unborn child. But she was also a victim: someone who had got mixed up in events and relationships that had led to her own tragic journey and the loss of some of her children. We wonder how she's coping and whether we'll ever have the chance to tell her that William is fine.

In all likelihood, the poor woman in the queue wasn't William's mother at all, but just as the school exercise triggered an emotional chain reaction for him, so the incident triggered an outpouring of emotions for Evie. We reasoned that it was her maternal instinct; that as William's mum, his *real* mum, Evie had become automatically protective. As the BT ad says, 'It's good to talk'. In fact, it's absolutely essential!

7

What about the other children?

Right from the beginning of the adoption process, our first concern was how adopting a child would affect our other children. That consideration influenced the kind of child we felt we could adopt. We were wary of adopting a child with chronic attachment difficulties, or extreme sexualised behaviour, because of the impact this could have on the others. We wanted there to be a large difference in age between the adopted child and the older three, so that there would be less likelihood of rivalry. We thought a child with disabilities would be less of a rival and evoke their compassion.

We knew that a disabled child would take up lots of our time, and it would therefore mean that we had less time for the others, but I think we underestimated this. William needs just about constant attention. Ed and Kate were almost at the stage of growing away from us when William joined the family, but Evie and I, being natural worriers, both feel that Robbie must have missed out in some ways. He hasn't excelled at school, his self-esteem has been rocky at times, and William picks on him and can wind him up. Not that we'd want Robbie to be any different to the way he is; he's popular and very, very funny (his George Bush impersonation, when he talks of penguins of mass destruction, reduces us to tears of laughter every time). He's kind, affectionate, rebellious, loud, and charming to strangers. He'll go far. But probably in a slightly different direction as a result of his life having been touched by William. Touched by, and at times dominated by.

This is the subject of occasional heart-to-hearts between Evie and me, usually when we have a rare night out together on our own, and end up spending the entire evening talking about the children, as we pick over green herb lamb and bhindi bhajee, washed down with a bottle of vino collapso.

Robbie is now 17. We give him an awful time – he's the only teenager left to worry about and nag. 'What time are you coming in tonight, Robbie?; 'Have you done your homework – those exams are just round the corner, you know. . .?; 'Could you unload the dishwasher, please Robbie?; 'Your bedroom is a tip, Robbie'.

Sometimes William and Robbie are great allies and conspire together, disappearing to cook and eat pot noodles in secret. At other times William is irrationally cruel and provocative, calling Robbie "big ears", and "curly hair" (his ears are unremarkable and his hair is too short to curl!). Silly and innocuous you might think, but William is a skilled wheedler. 'Don't touch Robbie's arm, William,' we'll say at teatime, but William *has* to extend his arm and pull at Robbie's sleeve, till Robbie moves out of reach. Then of course William has a tantrum. 'Robbie, come back, Robbie...'

I don't want to act the social worker in my family, but sometimes conversations with the kids seem to take a social-worky turn. I hope it's just me trying to be a good dad; checking things out. Robbie and I got talking the other day: 'It's good having a little brother,' he said, 'he's a nice wee chap.' Robbie lifts his repertoire of phrases from anywhere he fancies. Those he takes from me, like that one, have an affectionately mocking ring. 'I feel like we've helped him – given him a life, a family.'

'Like a duty, you mean?'

'No, no. We wanted to do it, didn't we?' He began drumming on his lap with his palms. Robbie can't sit still for long, and he's having a love affair with his drum kit. 'I liked him from the start. He's cute. He was very cute when he was little.' The thigh slapping reached a crescendo and he tossed his head about to the music in his head. 'I think I'm more aware of people with disabilities now, and the problems they face – they're just like us. It was hard for William not to have parents at the beginning and not being able to walk.' The drumming stopped for a few moments. 'It's amazing really, how positive he is,' he added, looking at me.

'Do you think he's changed you?' I asked.

The thigh slapping began again, slowly at first, but then the feet started going too. It's quite an art. 'I'm calmer now, more patient. He's helped me grow up. Remember how I used to lose my temper over nothing, get into such a rage?' He struck an invisible cymbal in the air.

'Yes. I was a bit like that myself as a child,' I said.

'I think of him as my brother,' continued Robbie. 'He is my brother. In fact in some ways I feel closer to William than to the others now. I suppose it's because they've moved on.' He drew his air drum playing to a spectacular close for the moment, with a final flourish. 'It's funny though, because at the same time I don't think I know him so well – my relationship with him is less natural than with the others.' He began beating out another rhythm with the ends of his fingers on the arm of the chair.

'Probably because they were around when you were born. They've always been there, part of you from the beginning, whereas William was his own self when he came.'

'Maybe, It isn't easy all the time of course. The thing I find most difficult is that he's ill such a lot.' The thigh slapping started again, gently.

I was quite surprised at this comment from Robbie. We are so used to William's migraines, upset tummies and constipation and I hadn't appreciated that Robbie found it so difficult.

'It annoys me,' he added.

'What, that he's ill?'

'No, he can't help that.' He stopped his drumming and twisted his baseball cap round so that it was back to front. 'It's just not fair on him. And it's a real shame he can't walk and play football and stuff. It's amazing how happy he is with all that. I feel really proud of him for the way he just gets on with life. I don't know how I'd be if it was me.' The drumming grew in volume, this time accompanied by a song, the words of which I couldn't make out.

'What about his temper tantrums?' I asked after a few moments.

'Yea, they're really annoying, but I used to lose my temper, remember?' I can immediately picture him screaming at the computer because it wouldn't do what he wanted it to. 'I think I understand how difficult it is to control yourself sometimes when you really want something and it doesn't work out. I feel sorry for him when he gets himself into a state. He's got a lot to put up with.'

'Does he embarrass you at all?' William can be loud and difficult in public.

Robbie looked at me with one of his "what are you talking about now?" expressions. He screwed up his face. 'NO. My friends *love* him – they think he's a little legend; that he's got a good personality. No one makes fun of him.' Robbie's band performed in the local church hall recently and Evie took William along to watch. Halfway through their set the lead singer paused and shouted, 'We love you William!' William was thrilled and went very pink. 'He's funny and loving. And I know he loves me, even when he's being rotten.' Robbie had a faraway look. 'I don't like his dribbling though,' he added, pulling a face. 'And I wish he could have more friends. When I met him from school the other day, his pal, Iain, just ignored him. William kept calling over to him across the road, but Iain just ignored him. I hate that.' Robbie got up and went over to the cupboard where he helped himself to another chocolate biscuit. He'll eat us out of house and home, as my mother used to say about me.

Earlier in the year we had decided to have a day out. We all love the sea. There's something cleansing to the spirit about the wrinkled, sparkling North Sea, and the yellow, gritty sand, shifting around the ankles as it's stirred by the exhausted incoming waves. You search the sky for the delicate terns, and follow their stretched beating wings till they fall upon a sand eel in the rippled shallows. A trip to the seaside seemed like such a good idea; held such promise. It was cloudy and it would be bracing once we got there. The fresh air would do us all good; blow the cobwebs away. 'Better out than in on a day like this,' one of us would say. It's a stock family phrase we all come out with on various occasions.

It was a bit of a drive. There were five of us: Evie at the wheel, and me in the front, William, Robbie, and Robbie's girlfriend Becca in the back. It might have been jealousy on William's part, but he began taunting Robbie.

'Robbie, you're smelly.'

'Gosh, look at those cows,' said Evie.

'Curly hair.' Everyone carried on as normal. 'Big ears.'

'Anyone like a crisp?' I asked leaning over to the back.

'I don't like you, Robbie.'

Robbie was tolerant, but it went on and on, and Evie

and I intervened with gentle reprimands, then sterner ones, then threats. They didn't make much of an impression. In fact, William seemed to see them as a bit of a challenge. He began touching Robbie who, after quietly asking him to stop, eventually got fed up and shouted at him. William kept on and we told him that if he didn't stop annoying Robbie, we'd stop the car and I would sit beside him instead of Robbie. Of course he carried on, so Evie pulled over and I got in the back beside William. Robbie moved to the side and Becca got in the front. Evie pulled out again. Hysteria erupted. William screamed and shouted. He told us he hated us all, especially Robbie. We tried singing. We tried stories. We tried bribes, but there was no shifting him. Eventually we got to the sea, and as we parked the car, so it started to gently rain.

'I don't want to get out of the car. I want to go home,' William screamed. We eased him, struggling, out of the car and into his wheelchair and wrestled to get his waterproofs on him. With great effort we got him down on the sand. It's hard work pushing a wheelchair on sand, but we tilted him back and got him onto the damp hard margin, near the sea. The waves were soft and had no spirit in them at all, the sky was grey and the rain crept about us in a fine mist. There were no terns. 'Leave me alone. Leave me alone!' he ordered.

'Okay, if that's what you want, love.'

We went off and strolled about, threw sticks for our old dog whose faculties are going, so that she can't see where they land and can't hear us helping her with clues. We generally mucked about and tried to be jolly. Robbie turned Becca over on the sand. We watched William out of the corner of an eye. He pushed himself towards the sea; he's surprisingly strong when determined. He pushed himself into the sea.

'Do you want to come with us, love? Don't get wet. Come on William, let's fly the kite.'

'Leave me alone.' The sea was washing round his tyres as they sank into the swirling, inundated sand.

Robbie approached him. 'C'mon, lets have a race against Becca.'

William played difficult to get at first, but eventually he began coming round, though he was still grumpy.

I started them off for the race. Robbie and William were given a head start. 'Ready, steady, wait for it...Go.' I put on my Wotshisname O'Sullivan voice for the commentary. 'And...they're off. And William Marsden is just in the lead, but he's being closely pursued by Bowling Becca, coming up on the stand side and, no, William is just about holding her off, but this is a spirited performance by the young filly and she might well take young William at the bend, but no, this is going to be a tight one, ladies and gentlemen, and at the half way mark it's still anybody's race...'

Robbie's trousers are too big. All of them. He likes bargain hunting, even if the bargains don't fit. Of course, the off-the-pelvis look is all the thing, so that the underwear can be seen, but Robbie's bargains are a bit extreme. Belts help to a degree, but the look he aims for suffers if his waistband is too constrained. As he receded away from us, so one hand desperately flailed about, trying to clutch at his slipping jeans, while the other tried hopelessly to propel the swerving wheelchair along the soft, sucking sand. It all happened very quickly: the jeans fell around Robbie's ankles, Robbie fell forwards, the wheelchair tipped over, and William lay trapped under his spinning wheels. Evie screamed and we both ran towards the scene. We righted the wheelchair: 'Are you all right, William? Are you okay?'

'Is that my blood?' William asked quietly. We all looked at the sand as a wave lapped over the crimson spots and they diffused into a pink puddle, and were gone. I used my hankie to dab at William's lightly cut lip. 'But I'm all right, I'm alright,' he kept saying. 'Did you see my blood, Robbie? Look at my blood!' William is so wrapped in protective cotton wool, that it was probably the first time his skin had been accidentally broken. He was a bit wobbly after his tumble, but the sight of his blood was a real treat for him. 'Did you see my blood, Becca? Look at Dad's hankie!' After that he was charming for the rest of the day, and as so often happens with him after a period of poor temper, he was doubly affectionate towards all of us.

* * *

'I think adopting William has made me more tolerant and patient.' Kate and I are driving along in the drizzle and the windscreen wipers make a scraping, screeching noise as they move over the glass. 'Oh, that noise drives me mad,' she snaps. We have been driving for a while.

'More tolerant, eh?'

'Oh, you! You know what I mean. I think it's good that we understand people with disabilities a bit more. I mean … before William was part of our family I'd have been a bit wary of speaking to someone with a disability, but not now.' She's about to put her earphones back in and immerse herself in her music again. I head her off at the pass.

'Okay, so it's been good for you. What about the effect on you emotionally, though?'

'Eh?'

'I mean, do you love him? Does it feel as if he's your brother?'

'Of course I do, you ninny. He's my brother, just the same as the other two. Of course he sometimes drives me mad, but so do the others.'

Kate was probably less affected by William when she was younger than the boys were. Because of her choir commitments she was regularly away from home overnight. He did go through a phase of being out to get her, though. 'You're so ugly, Kate. And you're smelly. I don't want to sit next to Kate.' Occasionally it reduced her to tears and she'd snap back about how nasty he could be, but it would be like water off a duck's back. 'What do you mean, I'm nasty?' As the only girl, Kate could be a bit isolated in the family, and sometimes the other boys were a bit slow in supporting her. I suppose that's life. Now though, William loves her, and when she comes home she does her bit in terms of role playing scenes from Pirates of the Caribbean with William, or whatever his latest craze is, and we've been with him to visit her at college, where she proudly introduced him to all her friends.

*　*　*

Ed left home for university when William was seven. William adores him. He longs to see him and weeps when Ed has to leave to catch the bus back after a weekend visit home. He gets jealous of Ed's girlfriend, and sometimes tries to come between them. He can give Ed a hard time too. Ed took him to rent a DVD a little while ago, and William made a fuss in the shop and screamed all the way home, so that Ed was drained and worn out. Then there was a cycle of remorse and regret, before Ed had to catch his bus.

Ed is William's Jedi master, and they have training sessions when Ed comes home, picking up each time from where they left off.

'Will you give me another training session, Ed?'

'Have you been studying the force, my young apprentice?'

'I've been trying, my master.'

'Very good. Let me see how well you handle your light sabre now.'

When I decided to write the story of our adoption, I asked Ed if I could talk with him about his memories and feelings. In response, he wrote me a note:

> *My first memory of William is when we all went to see him for the first time and he was sitting in his chair surrounded by Christmas presents.* (Ed was thirteen at

the time.) *As we walked in he gave me the biggest smile I have ever seen. I then remember us all taking him to the museum one day, and him eating one of those jars of mushy food in the café. Then the next thing was he was moving in with us! I was very surprised as to how quick it all happened. I was almost shocked when we brought him home after hardly seeing him, but I think you and Mum had seen him more often. I remember one thing from before I met William. It's bit embarrassing looking back: I dreamt that we went somewhere, a bit like dog kennels, and all the children were in cages on either side of us and that we went in, pointed to the one we wanted and then somehow saved it from that place.*

I'd asked Ed if he could tell me about the good things and the not so good things about adopting William. He misunderstood me and in his note compared how things might have been different if William had been our birth child rather than our adopted child. It didn't seem to enter his head that William might not have been part of the family. I later talked to Ed about this, and he explained that he didn't think that he'd really had any say about the decision to adopt, just as he hadn't had any say about having two birth siblings. But he felt William was as much a part of the family as the other children, and as fully his brother. He talked of William being happy and funny most of the time, and he said that because of William's cerebral palsy we had done things we would not otherwise have done, such as the physiotherapy exercises and Ed taking him to Beaver cub scouts. He felt this had been a good experience for him. During Ed's first year at university he did a project, which involved him being a wheelchair user for a day, with a fellow student filming him as he negotiated stairs and buses. Ed provided a voiceover commentary, and as we all watched the finished production, William nestled into Ed's shoulder, plainly touched that his hero and mentor would want to know how it feels to be him.

In his note, Ed mentioned the less positive aspects of having William as a brother, but again, he assumed the alternative to adopting him would have been to have him as a birth brother!

'William can be a lot of hard work, but so can any young kid. At least he can't run away! When I was younger it occasionally seemed like I did more than the others in terms of looking after him and playing with him, but I expect they feel the same, especially Robbie now that he's the only older one left.'

Ed is right about Evie and I expecting more of him than the others. He was older, more mature and more patient. Kate was away quite a lot with her music, and Robbie took a while to get into the "older and wiser brother" role though he's made up for it lately. Ed assures us he doesn't resent the responsibility he was given, but I'm not so sure. I'm fairly confident that he doesn't resent the act of adoption, and that it's more the oldest child syndrome, whereby he might have been under pressure to grow up rather quickly. This happens in all families where there is more than one child, but obviously in William's case, the burden on the older child is greater. I think it's a dynamic we're all still trying to work out.

> *I also worry about what he is going to think about his birth parents. I don't want him to get hurt if he makes contact with them. Now that I've written this note, it feels like I've said more negative things than positive ones, but that's not how I feel. Like all brothers and sisters, there are good memories and others that are not so good. I don't think the fact William is adopted is relevant at all.*

* * *

Ed now shares a flat with his girlfriend. He's moving on; finding his way in life. Their floor is strewn with clothes, empty mugs, and papers to do with their studies. The walls are covered with posters, arty clippings and sketches that Ed and his girlfriend have made. In amongst them, smiling out front is a photo of William. Neither Evie nor I remember giving it to Ed; he must have raided one of the shoe boxes where all the photos are stored, waiting to be put into albums. And funnily enough it's the same in Kate's room in the hall of residence. Among her timetables on the notice board and overlapping photos of her old school friends, is a photo of William, beaming into the room. In the common hall there's a poster saying "All boys are horrid, throw things at them." But one of Kate's neighbouring students has written 'except William' underneath, in response to William's protests during a visit.

You might assume that of all our children William would be the most stressful to care for. He is physically and emotionally dependent; he's socially isolated; he has health issues; his behaviour can be difficult; there are uncertainties about the future and so on. By comparison, our other children are reasonably independent now; they're turning into responsible, caring adults and their future prospects are as bright as we could wish for. But funnily enough, William isn't the one we usually worry about the most. We always know that William is safe; there aren't a lot of risks in his life – he's either with us, or he's at school or in some other carefully put together care arrangement or activity. The others are at large in the world and are exposed to pressures and influences beyond our control. Kate now lives in Manchester, and Evie and I exchange worried looks each time another murder there is reported in the news. Robbie goes off to rock festivals with his tent, and afterwards tells us graphic tales about the "mosh pit" and "crowd surfing", and the "really nice people" he's met. Ed doesn't show much inclination to be financially independent or to think about what he's going to do with his life after university.

I was talking recently to a friend whose daughter is disabled, and found that her experience was the same: 'We know exactly where we are with Susie – her needs are kind of straightforward, but Ben is a real worry. He's found it difficult to make friends at college, and I've got this mental picture of him just sitting in on his own at night. You hear stories of them getting really depressed, don't you?'

But the older kids aren't any less stressful when they are at home and we see them daily and can keep track of them a bit more easily. They come in late, create chaos with the clutter they randomly dump everywhere, contribute to the destruction of the planet (despite being passionate advocates for its salvation!) by leaving all sorts of electrical appliances switched on all over the place and rarely do anything to help around the house unless we go into nagging mode, when of course it all becomes even more stressful all round. They seem oblivious to the way Evie and I charge around juggling work with cooking, cleaning, dishes, washing and ironing and looking after William, while they recline in front of the TV or soak in the bath. I think I was the same at their age; it's hard to break out of the "parents are there to look after me" mindset, even well into adulthood. It's reassuring when we talk to friends who all have similar experiences, or at least they *say* they have.

My employer has a programme of health promotion, and offered blood pressure tests one lunchtime. So I abandoned my in-tray for a while, wolfed down my sandwich and apprehensively joined the queue. 'Just sit back in this nice comfy chair, Robert, and I'll strap this little monitor to your finger,' said the scented woman with the crackly white overall. 'There we go. Is that a permanent furrow on your brow?' She rippled with gentle laughter, and I tried to smile. 'That's right. Now, just close your eyes and think of something relaxing. One of your favourite places, perhaps? Or think of something that worries you and just imagine it going away...' I found myself thinking guiltily of the oldest three going away for the weekend, and of Evie, William and me having the house to ourselves. 'Oh, you've found the right spot there, Robert,' she said. 'The reading's gone right down!'

The worries concerning "The Family Business" aren't as straightforward as that, of course. The anxieties we have about William are different than they are about the others, not necessarily fewer. At the moment we seem to have reached a sort of plateau with William. His health is stable, his moods are fairly predictable, he's making reasonably good progress on all fronts, and almost every day he says, 'I love you Mum and Dad!' No doubt we'll have more stressful times ahead with William, just as we have had in the past. And if and when he does go out to rock concerts, or is whisked off by his pals for drinking sessions, I'm sure we'll be worried senseless. And we'll be even more worried if he doesn't manage to have a social life.

There is some research that shows that adoptions are less likely to turn out well if the adopted child is brought up alongside adopters' birth children. Our birth children have been heroes during our adoption journey. Maybe the age difference and William's physical dependency helped, in that he did not pose a threat to them. Whatever the reasons, they look upon him fully as their brother, and you can see the love that flows between them. I'd like to think he has enriched their lives – they say he has inspired them and brought them experiences they wouldn't have had. Who knows how they would have turned out if we had not adopted William? When we set off down the road to adoption we believed it would be rewarding for them, and we think and hope this has proved to be the case. They were great kids before we adopted William, and they're great kids now.

8

Inclusion and exclusion

William's social isolation is one of the hardest things for him to deal with and one of the most distressing for us. I've seen him call to children in the playground, and they ignore him. Even friends and family ignore him sometimes, when he asks something at mealtimes or during family get-togethers, not because they don't care about him, but because he can be immature and on a slightly different wavelength. We'll be talking about something we've heard on the news, and he'll ask why people close their eyes when they die! It's easy to overlook his need for social interaction, and in the family we all have to try hard to value what he is saying, to respond to him, and to help him know when, how and what sort of things to contribute to conversations. His peers are less sensitive and not so attuned to his needs. So they ignore him, or shun him or even ridicule him.

At the moment William is desperate to be friends with a classmate called David; a cool kid who looks good, plays football and is vaguely interested in Star Wars. We've had him round to play once or twice, but William's hunger for his friendship is not particularly returned, and recently

David's parents have declined invitations for him to come and play; they made an excuse so that he didn't come to William's last birthday party. They feel a bit awkward about it, but of course from David's point of view it is very understandable: William has a limited repertoire of things he is interested in and can do, and in public can be a source of embarrassment.

In the playground recently, William wheeled up to David, dribbling slightly, and asked if he'd like to come and play in a couple of days time. David evasively mumbled, 'Maybe next week,' and another boy, who was next to him muttered more loudly, 'Maybe next millennium,' and sniggered. It's heartbreaking. And of course, even when there is a friend who is prepared to engage with William, there is the question of whether the parents will be up for it. It's quite a thought having William round to play – there are steps to negotiate to get him into the house, feeding to worry about and toileting to think of. It is quite a trick to get the balance of friend and parent right. Either he has a friend whom he can relate to or there are sympathetic parents who feel able to manage him, but rarely is there a combination of both. We try to help William with his social skills, for example, suggesting that he needs to leave David alone for a time, and that maybe if he didn't feel hassled he'd be more inclined to play, but it's slow progress.

When William was first placed with us he went to a special pre-school nursery for children with disabilities. It involved an hour-long journey each way, and he had to go by taxi with an escort. The on-site therapy was excellent – there were physios on hand, speech therapists, hydrotherapy facilities, occupational therapy and anything else he needed. He was in a small class of about half a dozen and had lots of attention. The other children had various disabilities. Most were bright, but were very restricted physically, and I think only one had speech. When the time came for him to start school, we agonised over whether he would benefit most from continued specialist provision or from mainstream education, and in the end opted for some of each. So he went off to the special school for two days and to the local primary for the other three.

The local school of our choice was Catholic. It has a roll of about a hundred, with a warm, caring ethos. William's birth mother is Catholic and had stated that she wanted him to be brought up in the Catholic faith. In fighting for him to get a place, I'm afraid we exploited this fact, even going so far as to have him baptised. Remember the earlier reference to the need for children to have irrational advocates? Although maybe the phrase "bloody minded nuisances" is more in tune with the Scottish culture.

The arrangement involving the two schools worked fine, but as the school year wore on it felt more and more that he belonged at the local mainstream school, and would benefit most from a social point of view if he went there full time. There was something about the special school that seemed to label him as a problem needing special treatment. Of course he's "special," but first of all he's a child. It might sound a bit far fetched, but for much of the time we forget he's disabled. He's just William. It can sometimes feel as if he's seen as a "case" by the various therapists, and I think we're all at our happiest when the appointments diary is empty.

One of the therapists at the special school commented about his 'sometimes wilful behaviour'. She found him a bit precocious and spoilt (how dare she judge him at all!), and said that 'genes will out', meaning presumably that there was something about his background that meant he would never be a nice person. Evie was furious, and raged to me about the stupidity of people who should know better in view of William's history of ill health, change, loss and trauma. She was a bit more polite to the therapist, but I think she made her point! So, gradually we decided that he should go to the local primary on a full-time basis and that's what happened after the first year.

The local school is brilliant at including William as far as they can. The social isolation has become more of a problem as he has got physically bigger and less easy to lug about, and he has got left behind a bit by his peers who are maturing at a faster rate than he is. Over the last year he has talked with affection about his memories of the special school – maybe it was easier for him socially, and he has missed out on peer support from other children with disabilities. Maybe he'll go to specialist provision again in the future?

Whilst the local school is really good, there are always issues, problems and little incidents to wrestle with, as there are for any child, but on a greater scale. At a recent parents' evening, Evie was saying to William's teacher how pleased we were with his progress. The staff all work very hard on William's behalf and we try to give them positive feedback.

'Yes,' said the teacher. 'He could improve some more, but we just don't know, do we. He might not improve at all, might he?'

We had a laugh about it afterwards. It seemed such an odd thing to say. We don't expect William to be an intellectual high flyer, but he is making academic progress at school and there is no sign that this will suddenly stop.

The phrase "developmentally delayed" is a little dangerous. It can imply that things are running late, but that we'll get there in the end. We want William to try and reach his potential, that's all. If I'm honest, I'd say that at one point it seemed important to me that he should walk and read fluently and add up, but now I'm wiser and accept that he will do what he will do, and that achievement of conventional goals is neither here nor there.

Because of his social isolation, Evie and I find ourselves

taking on the role of friend as well as parent. When children are very young, their parents are their first playmates, but as they grow older, peers and siblings take over and it's a joy to see children going off into fantasy worlds of their own, with a few toys and a lot of imagination. With William we've had to carry on as his playmates. Most evenings before he goes to bed he pleads with me to act out some scenario or other with him:

'Can we have a wrestle, dad?'

It's usually the last thing I feel like after we've finished tea and I've just sunk into a chair and picked up the Radio Times to see what might be on later.

'Okay, just a quick one, though – it is your bedtime. What are we going to do?' I say, trying to sound enthusiastic

'Let's do *Lord of the Rings*,' he'll say, beginning to thrash about in excitement.

'Okay, Mr Frodo.' I'll help him out of his chair and tell him to crawl through to his room – that's where we keep all the weapons, and the journey, which is part of the game, is good exercise! 'Watch out – here come the trolls, Mr Frodo,' I'll shout in a panic-filled voice.

'I'm Mr William, Sam,' he'll say, trying to get onto all fours. It's funny the way he always wants to hang on to his own identity.

'I'm sorry, Mr William,' I say, in a vaguely Somerset Samwise Gamgee accent, 'but we need to fly, fly – here they come!' And we both set off to get our weapons. (When our older three were younger, ours was a weapon-free house. We went on CND marches and harped on to them about non-violence! But for some reason, we've let William acquire all sorts of swords, spears and yes, even guns. Maybe he needs them as aids to assertiveness in his games?)

And then William tries to brandish a sword on all fours, and the imaginary arrows start flying. We both make zippy noises as they pierce the air and whistle past our ears, and we take turns getting wounded.

Another night it will be James Bond. 'So Mr Bond, we meet again for the last time,' I say in a smooth, Blofeld-type voice. 'Tell my pet sharks that their dinner is ready, Oddjob, 007 will be with them soon! '

'The name's Mr William, and I'm 003! I'm going to get you Blofeld,' and William points his gun from a half sitting position. I die spectacularly and in great pain.

Or *Star Wars*: 'Come, young Skywalker,' I say in my raspy, evil emperor voice, 'join me on the dark side and together we'll rule the universe.'

'I'll never join you,' William shouts lunging with his light sabre. 'And my name is William.'

Or Harry Potter. 'Expelliamus,' he'll shout, pointing a makeshift wand at me, and I'll have to keel over, struck down by some dreadful curse.

'I'll get you for that, Potter,' I'll retort, writhing on the ground.

'Oh yea, Malfoy. And the name is William...'

Sometimes, it feels as if he gets too engrossed. I tuck him up in bed with an imaginary Crabbe and Goyle (who have joined Gryffindor House and are now goodies). I have to pretend to be them snoring as I close the door, and next morning as soon as he's awake they are there again, waking up next to him. 'Pretend Crabbe and Goyle are just waking up, Dad, and one of them has had a scary dream and I've had to tell him to shut up and...' It can be hard to get him back into the real world. Most kids would act out all these scenarios with their pals, but for the most part, that's just not an option for William – other children get bored and frustrated at his limitations and immaturity. My acting skills have improved dramatically over the last few years, but I've got housemaid's knee as a result of being on all fours so much! Ed, Robbie and Kate take their turns too, but we don't like to ask too much of them.

Inclusion is the social policy mantra at the moment, driven by a mixture of economics and ideals. Specialist education provision is very expensive and can lead to the marginalisation and isolation of children with disabilities. But a disabled child is not necessarily included just because he or she is enrolled in a mainstream school or activity. Unless they are socially accepted and involved, children with disabilities can find themselves ostracised and very lonely. I know of one young person who was educated in a mainstream high school and ended up asking to be moved to a special school because he felt so isolated. He was a bright, articulate boy who very bravely stood up at assembly one day and told the whole school how he felt and why he was moving. Brings a lump to your throat just thinking about it. William isn't at that stage yet. He still likes school, and has enough social interaction to keep him going; he's cute, so the older girls make a fuss of him; he's funny, so the younger boys laugh with him; some children like to push him around in his wheelchair, though it's much better for him if they don't! But, with one or two exceptions, his peers don't fully engage with him.

At a school fair the other evening, Evie was queuing up with William for a burger, and a classmate in front of her told his friend, who is not a pupil at the same school, just to ignore 'that boy in the wheelchair' (William was trying to introduce himself). Evie was seething, but the incident did lead to an invitation to come and play at the house of another classmate, whose mother was behind Evie in the queue and had heard everything. As the old saying goes, children can be very cruel.

It's very difficult to know what to do about promoting inclusion. As parents we chip away and persevere with the friendships, and so far William's social needs are just about being met. It's possible that his social life will improve as he grows older and relationships become more verbal than physical, but who knows? At the moment he isn't very confident physically, and doesn't like to take risks. I wrote a story for him about a wheelchair user who built a tree house in the woods with some friends – I thought I'd go for an adventurous scenario and encourage him to get away from the stereotypes. I touched on inclusion issues, risk-taking, independence and the ups and downs of friendships. He loved the story, but there's not much sign of him taking any more risks! Or articulating to his friends how he feels about being socially isolated. I think he's going to have to tell them as he grows older, so that he can try and ensure for himself that his needs are met. He did ask one younger friend why he didn't play with him at break times anymore, and the friend told him it was because he liked to run around, and William just couldn't keep up. The dawn of insight is a painful process.

A few schools use a concept called "circle of friends," in which the whole class is involved in looking at how to address issues like including children with disabilities or tackling bad behaviour. Maybe we should be taking the lead and pushing the school a bit more, but it all takes time and energy to get these things going ...

We try to help William relate both to the able bodied world and to the disability world. He goes to riding for the disabled and he goes to a Saturday morning sports club for children with disabilities. We have to stay with him in case he needs to be lifted. We think it is good for him to mix with other disabled children so that he realises he is not alone, and gets some sense of support. This might become more important when he is older. He's been on wheelchair skills training courses, and seems gradually to be gaining an identity, a pride even, in being a wheelchair user who can do some things independently.

We know some parents who insist on their disabled children being included as fully as possible and who believe, for example, that the specialist sports club is an insult to their children because it segregates them from others. Perhaps they are right and that is the only way to change society, but some of our attempts at pushing inclusion have had mixed results in terms of the quality of William's experience. We enrolled him into the Beaver Scouts but the leaders said that either Evie or I had to accompany him to the weekly meetings. We looked at the Scout movement's website and found an impressive equal opportunities policy. But the practice is different in reality. William didn't particularly want his mum or dad to go with him to Beavers; none of the other children were accompanied by their parents, but he did need more help than the leaders could offer, and every organisation, school, club or whatever, has a "no lifting" policy for health and safety reasons, which seems to us to be simply a denial of a problem. It is not possible to care for William without lifting and handling him!

We had various meetings with senior scout leaders. As I arrived for one, I found the area organiser chain smoking outside the scout hut, obviously dreading this encounter with a vocal parent over equal opportunities. We edged our way towards a solution. Ed would take William to the meetings, then a senior scout would give him one-to-one attention. We would make sure he went to the loo beforehand, and it was agreed that he would spend the meetings in his wheelchair, so that he would not need to be lifted. The organisers tried to find activities that William could join in with, but with his poor fine motor skills, limited sight and confinement to the wheelchair, it wasn't easy, and in some ways not fair to the other very active children. Then the senior scout helper left and the term came to an end. I'm afraid we just didn't find the energy to face all the hassle again the following term. William still talks of wanting to go back.

In theory, just about everyone supports the idea of social inclusion, but not many people have the time to make it happen. The sports club William goes to is poorly run. Few children go to it because it is not well publicised, the sessional staff who run it are not trained in managing children with disabilities, parents are not involved in working out the programme and so on. It's almost a disaster, and everyone we speak to agrees. 'Yes, you should phone so and so…why don't you parents get together and set down the issues…there's a regional meeting about sport coming up next month – you should get involved in that.' Yes, we should do all of those things, but it is so hard finding the time and energy. We did write a letter of complaint containing constructive suggestions, but didn't get a reply. What we'd really, really like is for someone to do it for us. Just a simple thing like identifying a volunteer to take William to cubs would make such a difference to his life and to ours, but you have to find the volunteer, train him or her, check liability issues, undertake police checks and provide support. Then they can't come one week and everything falls apart, or they move on to other things.

Some of the gestures at inclusion are painful. Once a year William goes along to the inter-school sports day. All the sports are geared for physically able children. Sport is about physical ability, speed and athleticism. When he was younger William was desperate to take part. Evie lined up on the starting line with the other boys and pushed him down the fifty-meter dash. Everyone was very kind and encouraging, but the experience was excruciating and denied the reality of William's disability. The next year he wanted to do it again, but Evie got too upset at the silliness of it all, and by William's lack of dignity and independence, so a heroic friend pushed him instead. We've managed to avoid the races since and confined William's participation to spectating. Yes, I know we should be pressing the school to develop sports he can take an active part in.

Probably the most inclusive activity for William outside school is swimming. He can just about manage a length of the pool without any buoyancy aids, though his stroke is a bit like that of a two-toed sloth, rolling about in what seems to strangers to be a very alarming manner. I've got the knack of knowing when drowning is imminent and pulling him back to the surface! The trouble is that he giggles at the slightest provocation, and underwater giggling is a hazardous business. Everyone knows him at the swimming pool, and by the time he's conversed with them all it takes us ages to get in and out. Swimming gives him a wonderful freedom and puts him on a par with his peers. 'Go away Daddy, I'll be fine,' he tells me. 'No, further away – go down the deep end and enjoy yourself.' And I try to hide behind other swimmers, at rescuing distance, so that I can be ready to swim over and ease him to the surface if he begins to sink. Meantime he tries to muscle in on other children's games with varying success. Sometimes they move away, sometimes they tolerate him, but sometimes they adapt their game and include him. A few get alarmed about the way he disappears below the surface in a gurgling spiral of bubbles, and touchingly insist on holding him up. He doesn't object, though he can manage perfectly well most of the time.

Occasionally there are physical barriers to inclusion for William, or at least for his wheelchair. He cannot go to some school events at the local museum because there are stairs; there are also steps up to the church where end of term services are sometimes held. But on the whole access to buildings is becoming easier. Getting into toilets can be tricky. We never go anywhere without William's urine bottle, though attempting to use it in the car usually brings on a case of the "sun roof terrors!"

Some things are becoming more of a problem now that he is getting bigger. Up to the age of eight, he was small and light enough to be able to fit into a child carrier that strapped to my back, and we used to go for walks through woodland and along rocky shores, which we all loved. But that's no longer possible, so it's a case of searching for wheelchair-friendly walks or taking turns – one of us going off for a walk while the other one does something else with William. Wherever we go people are incredibly friendly and helpful. During a Spring trip to the small Scottish island of Ulva, various burly passengers helped to lift William and his chair into the tiny passenger ferry for the crossing, and he was transported by Landrover over the roadless island to the small church for the Easter service. On the return crossing, the ferryman churned up the water in tight spiralling circles especially for William till he was crying with the happy thrill of it all.

I think as time goes on inclusion will be more of a challenge. When he was small he was a buggy-user and his disability was less obvious; he was easy to lift and carry and life went on as normal. Now the actual mechanics of inclusion are more difficult, and lord knows how they will be if he grows to six foot and weighs twelve stone! To be an adolescent will be an awfully big adventure.

9

What about our needs?

It's stating the obvious, but it's a fact: adoption changes your life! You can't just absorb a child into your family without changing your lifestyle. You have to give up certain things, you have to make financial adjustments, you have to cope with emotional pressures and deal with changing relationships. I think we grossly underestimated the impact adoption would have on our lives – probably part of the "it won't happen to us" syndrome. The social worker tells you about the possible horrors that could lie ahead, such as attachment problems, behavioural difficulties, uncertain prognoses and so on. You take it all in, but you harbour an assumption that you will be different from everyone else who has struggled with these things; you will buck the trend. We were a happy family of five, trundling merrily along. We had trips away, holidays in the sun, meals in restaurants. We had an allotment, we had a decent income and we had freedom. If we'd wanted we could have moved house to another part of the country – the world even – in search of change or challenge or whatever. Adopting William was one of our better life choices. We became a happy family of six. But the decision affected just about every waking minute of our lives and many of the sleeping ones too!

At least we didn't have legal worries when William came to live with us. He was "free" for adoption. In other words the court had made a special order which meant that the local authority could place him for adoption without further reference to his birth family. After he had lived with us for a time, we submitted an application to our local court for the finalisation of the adoption. Adopters do not always have such an easy ride. If the birth parent opposes the adoption, the court process becomes adversarial. So just when the new family is coming together, with all the associated emotional upheaval, there is the background anxiety of legal uncertainty. It can take weeks to get court dates, and even then there can be adjournments and delays. The court process itself can be a costly legal game of point scoring between lawyers and the outcome can be determined on technicalities. No one could argue against civil rights and due legal process, but there must be a better, speedier, more child-centred way of determining a child's future.

All the minor adjustment we had to make after William moved in added up. We gave up those personalised little letters that used to go with Christmas cards, and resorted to the much-mocked "round robin", like this extract from 2005:

Hogwarts School of Wizardry and Witchcraft

My Dear Albus,
Minerva here, on the quill. Thank you for your Owl. We are all so sorry that you won't be able to join us for Christmas. Still, at least in Azkaban you won't have to watch The Great Escape on TV. I hope the following information about the progress of some of the newer students will help you keep your spirits up.

As you know we have a new house at Hogwarts, called the House of Marsden. The head of house is Professor Evie, who is the school's new Professor of Fair Trade and Organic Consumption. Sadly, she's a witch who's cursed. Yes, poor Professor Evie suffers from the dropsy curse. Only on Friday she fell outside Glasgow railway station and immediately acquired 17 additional multi-coloured chins and a pair of bruised knees. The arnica potion appears to be working slowly, certainly more effective than the loud embarrassing counter curses she utters when she falls. We have named a local walk after her – The Falls of Evie – a bit like the Falls of Lenny but more to the south. Her organic efforts are legendary – we are not allowed to breathe the air unless it has been certified as wholly organic.

Then there's Robert. He's a bit like a slimmed-down version of our old friend Hagrid, except that he's rather greyer and his hair is quite thin. Sadly he's got the nagging curse and goes on at the younger students mercilessly. He can be quite useful around the school, though. He brings home money, cooks and cleans a bit, that sort of thing. He struggles on at work, trying to cope with the monthly reorganisation. (It's like those constantly moving staircases, he says, except you're even less sure where you might end up.)

Young Ed is 19 and has a case of the dreadlocks, which he got on a Spanish beach in the summer. I must say he bears them with remarkable fortitude and bravery. He is in his second year at university doing Art, or is it Defence against the Dark Arts? He is learning to drive in the family's Panda, Professor Evie's Ford Anglia having bitten the dust in the 1970s. How time flies (a bit like the Anglia)!

Kate is now 17 and suffers from the "loseitandbeuntidy" curse. She has tried the counter-charm, i.e. standing in the middle of her room with her violin bow, going swish and flick, but the results are rather disappointing. She occasionally creates a little eddy of dust, but that is all.

Young Robbie (15) repels dementors (and parents) very effectively by banging on his drum kit. His band won a battle of the bands recently – a mixed blessing, since he is now convinced that stardom is just around the corner and that standard grades (O.W.L.S. to you) are unnecessary. Somehow he seems to have been infected with a growth potion. Unless we can find an antidote, this time next year his curly locks will be brushing the ceiling.

William (8) has benefited from the magic of medicine this year. He has had a Baclofen pump inserted under his skin, to release a drug to prevent the muscles of his legs contracting too much. He crawls well, self-propels in his wheelchair, and can transfer from bed to wheelchair now. He also swims like a magical creature. He can swim a whole length of the local swimming pool, which is infested with blast-ended screwts and flubberworms. He's keen on that funny Griffindor pupil, Harry Potter, and we've read all the books to him this year (not that you'd ever have guessed).
Etc...
Love,
Minerva McGonnagal

* * *

We gave up the round robin after listening to a scathing attack on the genre on Radio 4. So this year, friends just got signed cards. We struggled to keep the allotment going and eventually gave it up after a few months when it became hard to locate the King Edwards amongst the weeds. I get a kick out of watching vegetables grow from seeds the size of grains of sand, so in the absence of an allotment we now have various holes in our lawn where broad beans, lettuces, leeks and potatoes reach for the sun. The house became even less clean and tidy; the piles of un-ironed washing grew; Evie and I found we had less time together; outings and holidays had to be more carefully planned. One solution to all these extra demands would have been a thirty-hour day, but in the absence of this we looked for a mixture of informal support, formal support from agencies, financial help, and changes in the way we organised our lives. Some forms of help came almost automatically with William, and other assistance came more slowly, and sometimes only after battles.

Time is the most precious resource. When William moved in, Evie and I both got adoption leave. In Evie's case, this involved a mixture of paid and unpaid leave for a year from her part-time job. As our other children were aged fourteen, twelve and ten at that time, it was important that we had time to see to everyone's needs during this period of upheaval and adjustment. I got five days paid adoption leave, which I spread over about three weeks. This doesn't sound much but it was a great help, and I topped it up with annual leave to ease us all through the transition.

Another type of help that kicked in right away was William's Disability Living Allowance (DLA), to help with mobility costs and additional care arising from his disability. This is available to all children with disabilities, not just those who have been adopted. We also have an adoption allowance. This is a weekly sum paid to adopters, subject to means testing and review, in relation to certain children who are "hard to place". The amount depends on the age of the child, and in our case this works out to about £80 per week. The allowance is intended to cover the additional costs associated with adopting a child with special needs who would otherwise be difficult to place for adoption. It's something else to feel guilty about. But there is no financial gain in adoption! Evie's income fell because she cut her hours of work in order to care for William. Her career prospects all but disappeared. We pay for after school care for William, private massage, a private physio programme and training in lifting and handling. We've also paid a contribution to a house extension, so that William can have an en-suite bathroom suitable for his needs. It seems Scotland is the only country in Europe which charges parents for house adaptations carried out by local authorities for children with disabilities. We're currently waiting for the installation of ramps to the house, and will have to pay 50 per cent towards the cost. The latest estimate comes to nearly £10,000 to ramp two small steps, so we've told the council to put the work on hold for now! I have a feeling that contractors see the potential of easy money when they land a council contract.

Apparently some studies show that it costs about three times as much to bring up a child with disabilities than it does to bring up other children. We've never sat down to work it out, but I suspect if we added up things like extra heating costs (William needs to be kept warm) laundry costs (William is always being sick), nappies (needed in some cases for life), and so on, that figure wouldn't be far from the truth. Then there are child care costs, generally higher than for other children, holidays where special facilities might be needed, and miscellaneous bits of equipment and help. We're currently planning to lease or buy an adapted vehicle, which will cost far more than the DLA.

There is awkwardness in talking about financial matters. Some would say that the notion of an adoption allowance under any circumstances is not appropriate – after all, birth parents don't get paid for having children, so why should adopters? We'd have gone ahead with the adoption regardless of whether William came with or without an allowance, but the allowance has definitely made life just a little easier, and for some families could make the difference about whether life is manageable or not. There are lots of children waiting to be adopted, and if allowances will help some of them to get placed, then that is justification enough.

One interesting development in recent years has been the introduction of specialist fostering schemes for children who are "difficult to place". Some of these have been pioneered by the growing independent sector, with agencies charging local authorities up to £1,500 per week for a placement, and carers themselves sometimes receiving fees of several hundred pounds a week. Such schemes can offer carers an alternative to employment, which is fine if it means that children who would otherwise live in institutions, which can cost up to £5,000 a week, can be brought up by families in the community. But what will be the knock-on impact for adoption? Once potential adopters work out that if they foster instead, they could receive an income that would enable them to give up work, will anyone in their right mind wish to adopt a child with disabilities? The obvious conclusion must be that the number of adoptions will decline, despite it being the option that most closely resembles being brought up by birth families, and which has the most successful outcomes. Life would certainly have been easier if Evie had been able to give up work, or if I had been able to reduce my hours, but the loss in income would have been tricky to manage.

It would be easy for the most altruistic of adopters to get into a state about things being unfair; they could feel resentful of foster carers who get paid for bringing up children, and about the lottery of support that is around. In Scotland there are thirty-two local authorities and they each have a different adoption allowance scheme, so that a child might attract an allowance in one part of Scotland, but not in another. If adoption is to be a serious element of the nation's childcare strategy, these anomalies need to be resolved.

There are new regulations, which give the parents of a child with disabilities the right to apply for flexible working arrangements. Evie now works annualised hours, so that as long as her hours of work add up at the end of the year, she can work flexibly. She can bank hours one week and work less the next week, so she can get William to the various appointments he has or be at home with him if he is unwell.

I now work at home one day a week. For people who have never worked at home this might sound like a cushy little number, but it is the most stressful day of my week. I get William up and off to school, so that Evie can do a long day at work; then it's a rush of phone calls, report writing, a sea of emails, without the luxury of people coming in to distract you with queries, gossip and the offer of chocolate biscuits. There's a personal pressure to get as much done as possible, with an eye on the clock for the time to meet William from school.

I get him home and settled in front of the computer or TV and get back to work. But I'm usually interrupted at various points because he's dropped a toy or got himself onto the wrong website or needs a pee, so I have the dual role of parent and worker to juggle. Then I feel obliged to do some more work in the evening, after I've cooked the family's tea and cleared up and got William to bed. It's not particularly amusing when colleagues say, 'Oh, we can't meet tomorrow, can we, because you don't work on Wednesdays,' and I have to remind them that I *do* work on Wednesdays, probably a lot more productively than other days, but that I work at *home*. As a paranoid sort of person, I'm sure they talk together about the self-imposed stress in our lives. 'They must have known what they were taking on at the beginning. It's not as if they didn't have a choice, is it?' And of course they are right, though I bristle at what can feel like something close to discrimination of parents who adopt children with disabilities; a small but oppressed minority group!

William goes to a private mainstream after-school club once a week and for some half-days during holiday periods. This enables us to work and gives him social contact with other children. It's an excellent set-up; the staff have a positive "can do" culture, and just get on with the lifting and handling and all the other minutiae that are needed to care for William properly. Nothing is a problem for them, and William is more truly "included" there than just about anywhere else.

Over time we have found out about other forms of practical help available to children with disabilities. For example, if you adapt your house for a disabled person you can get a reduction in your council tax. If someone in the household is registered as blind, though not partially sighted, like William, you can get a discount in the cost of a TV licence. If you go to the cinema or the swimming pool, the "carer" can get a reduced entry charge. It would be great to have a handbook of all these benefits. Maybe there is one, but we haven't found it yet.

Some benefits are a mixed blessing. Despite having a disabled parking badge we have managed to get three parking tickets in the last few weeks; once because a tyre was a fraction of an inch inside an area reserved for resident permit holders, even though there were no other cars parked in the street at the time; another when we misinterpreted the restricted parking sign; and once because our badge had expired (there's no reminder). The last two times we were taking William to hospital, and both times we appealed, but without success. The law can be a faceless bureaucrat!

William has a travel pass that enables him and his "attendant" to travel free on the local buses. We don't make much use of it because the car is so much easier, but recently Evie decided to take William to a hydrotherapy session at the regional hospital by bus because Ed needed to borrow the car. Not all our local buses are accessible for wheelchairs, so Evie phoned up beforehand to check on the timings. She had to get an earlier bus than she'd hoped, and when it pulled up in the engulfing drizzle she found it wasn't accessible after all. The driver helped her haul William and his wheelchair up the steps, and there was just enough room to wedge him in beside the front seat. The bus was quite busy and William chatted away to his fellow passengers as they got on and off, slightly sauna-like now, with the rising vapour from damp coats and umbrellas. One rather toothy middle-aged man with well-groomed raven-black hair passed the time of day for a few stops, and was obviously quite taken with William.

The journey to the hospital took about an hour and the driver helped William and Evie off at the other end. They idled away an hour in the hospital café, William poring over the latest *Beano*, before heading to the pool, only to be told on arrival that the session was cancelled because the previous child had had a bowel movement in the water and it would take twenty-four hours to clear. What can you do other than smile and say, 'Never mind, we'll be here again next week!'

A wheelchair-accessible bus wasn't due for two hours, so Evie decided to take the next "ordinary" bus, and the driver obligingly helped her aboard again. William's newfound toothy friend with the raven hair joined the bus at the point he'd been dropped off earlier. In the intervening hours he'd had a large liquid lunch, and he breathed alcohol and stale tobacco over William and Evie, as he leaned over the back of the seat talking about the cruelty of life, his black hair, plainly a wig, slipping around his skull as he periodically scratched himself. 'But you're a fine wee lad, and here's a pound for you, and God bless,' he said, as he pushed a coin into William's hand and gave his knuckles a kiss. As he disembarked, he offered to help Evie off the bus, but it was still a good few miles before her stop. He gave them a cheery wave as he stumbled down the steps, and they last saw him groping in the gutter for his hairpiece as the bus drew away, back out into the misty rain.

'Did you have a good day?' I asked when I got home. William showed me his pound.

'Is this enough for a Star Wars toy?'

'Not quite. You could put it in your moneybox.'

'What happens to people when they get drunk, Dad?' Questions on this theme came for most of the evening as he tried to work it out.

Experiences on public transport aren't always the stuff of amusing anecdotes, though. We have a disabled adult friend with an electric wheelchair who regularly travels to town by bus. She always phones to check the timings of the wheelchair-accessible bus, but more often than not, when it pulls up she finds it has been substituted for one that she can't board. So she has to wait for the next one, or the one after that: sometimes up to two hours. Not much fun when you're stranded on the cold wet streets of Edinburgh.

Curiously, some help was put in place without our having asked for it. We were told that because we had a child with disabilities we were "entitled" to a home help from the local authority, and for several years now someone has come for two hours a week to do some ironing and cleaning. William is usually at school when she comes so she has little direct contact with him. In some ways the arrangement is more of a strain for us than a help; we have to be reasonably tidy and organised and the home help can't be left in the house alone, so Evie has to plan her own working hours around her. We'd much rather have help more directly geared to William's needs: a befriender or a baby-sitter, or "direct payments", a cash payment that is an alternative to service provision and would enable us to employ a helper occasionally. We've been on a waiting list for direct payments for about a year – apparently it is not possible simply to transfer funds from the home care budget. In the meantime, the home help continues to come each week; we are reluctant to give up the one practical form of help we receive until another is in the pipeline. As a home care service user, William is periodically invited to social events arranged by the local office. These include sherry parties and a recent excursion to see the film, *Ladies in Lavender*. We declined the invitations on his behalf. We're told he's the only child in the area still receiving a home help service; the invitations, presumably churned out by computer, give the notion of inclusion a different spin!

Last year William's OT decided he would benefit from a specialist tricycle. She produced a brochure and we noticed that it would cost about £1,000. 'But don't worry,' she said, 'I'll try and get some financial help from a Trust.' We filled in various forms and gave details of our income, and to our surprise a Trust did come up with the funding. In fact, the trike was part-financed by a trust fund set up by David and Victoria Beckham, which William was very thrilled about. We had a call one day to say that David wouldn't be able to speak to William on the phone after all, because of his busy schedule. It was the first we'd heard of any possible call, and we spent some time researching the team David played for and the names of his children, in case he called after all. It would be just like me to lift the phone and say, 'David who? I think you must have the wrong number!' During the first outing on the trike, which William calls "the Beckham", half the street came out to cheer him on! It's been great to see him charging around the playground with the other kids, and knowing that the exercise is good for his muscles.

We get tremendous support from our friends. When William was baptised we recruited two wonderful friends –

Anne and Marion – as Catholic godparents, alongside the adoptive parents of his two birth brothers. In fact Marion arranged the baptism for us in her church, as the local priest put up various obstacles because neither Evie nor I are Catholics. Marion takes her Catholicism seriously; she goes to mass regularly, places lighted candles next to the Blessed Virgin, prays to St Anthony when she loses things, and swears and curses like a trooper in unguarded moments. Anne was a former nun, but later found love and had three children. She has an elegant piety about her when in church, but gets tipsy and voluble on half a glass of red wine. She knows just about everything there is to know about Catholicism, but no advice is foolproof.

'William's friend is going to his first communion next week, Anne. What should we get him?'

'Oh, just a gesture – a moral book or something like that. Maybe you could just put another thimbleful of that nice red wine in my glass, my dear?'

In fact the moral book looked a bit sad next to the pile of expensive electronic games and wads of banknotes, and didn't elicit unconfined joy from the recipient.

Anne and her husband, Jim, take William for an overnight every couple of months or so, and Marion and her husband entertain him the following day and bring him home. He adores them all, and tells us he would much rather live with Anne and Jim than with us! It's wonderful to sit in the house, in the silence, just occasionally on a Sunday morning, flicking through the Sunday supplements and sipping fresh coffee. But we usually end up talking about William and the other children, and after a short while the house can feel very empty without him. It's amazing how often these little islands of respite don't work out, though: William is ill so we have to cancel; we once headed off to stay with friends, but the road was blocked by an accident and we had to turn back and come home; another time we decided to stay in Edinburgh with William to give us all a break, but it was Saint Valentine's Day and all the decent hotels were booked up. We ended up in a seedy B and B with a lumpy bed and a greasy breakfast in the morning. Memorable, but not quite the luxurious treat we'd envisaged!

We have other friends who help with William's physiotherapy exercises, coming every week for an hour or so to work through a programme of stretching, moving and fine motor skill development. William is usually resistant at first, not wanting to come off the computer or switch off the TV, but Joan and Julian just take charge in a matter of fact way and we leave them to it. Soon the three of them are giggling away, Joan and Julian having turned the exercises into games of fun. It's so helpful to be able to hand over a bit of the therapeutic work to friends who are so reliable and capable.

We have some friends who baby-sit. Sorry, William hates that expression – I should say boy-sit, and as the other children have got older they have tended to do that occasionally. We don't like to ask them often though, and as we age it seems more and more of an effort to go out anyway. A night in with a takeaway and a bottle of wine is much more relaxing. Much of our evening child care is needed for work-related evening meetings. We assumed William knew what we were up to till one day he asked Evie, 'What are those ducks doing, Mum?'

'They're mating, William.' Honesty is the best policy.

'Is that what you do when you go out in the evenings? Mating?'

'What?' Evie wondered if he'd picked up some smutty playground talk.

'You know all those matings you're always at?'

'No William, honey. No, those are *meetings*. They're quite different; places where people talk to each other to try and sort out problems. The ducks here are making babies.'

'Oh.'

Evie has a great circle of women friends, some of whom happen to be nurses, physiotherapists and social workers. She gets a lot of support through talking to them, not just about William, but about life, the universe and everything. It's important to keep things in perspective!

But most of the practical and emotional support Evie and I get and need comes from each other. We take turns going off for the odd weekend; Evie to sew, drink herbal tea and put the world to rights with old friends, and I for periods of solitude, wet walks and the odd glass of malt over a good book.

The social worker at the adoption society through which we adopted William kept in touch with us for some months after William was first placed, and then the contact came to a natural end. We still see her and other staff from the society at social events they organise. Sometimes the society offers training courses and support groups. Evie has been to the odd training event, but on the whole we are fairly self-sufficient. My work steeps me in adoption and child care to the point where I feel fairly saturated.

We do get stuck fairly frequently over issues like interpreting William's behaviour, thinking through contact arrangements, wondering how to tackle social isolation and so on, but William is so unique that it seems best just to try and work it out together. However, the time may yet come when we need professional support, and no matter how much knowledge you might have, it can sometimes be very helpful to get an objective perspective to help you stand back. It is reassuring to know there are lots of national and local agencies out there to provide help and support should the need arise. At the moment, though, we most value those little islands of time when we hand William over to the care of others for short periods, and we can just be still for a few hours, at the end of which it's always great to see him back home again.

Sometimes simple things can become very complicated

because of William's needs. Evie recently drove to the railway station to meet her mother off a train. She had William with her in his wheelchair, and he announced that he needed to go to the loo (always a bit of a performance). As she emerged from the public conveniences the tannoy announced that her mum's train would be pulling into a different platform from the scheduled one. She found the platform and discovered that the lift leading to it was out of order. She dashed to the station office, and two helpful porters were assigned to help her. But the train pulled in to the original platform after all. 'Never you mind, hen, we'll find her. What does she look like?' the porters asked.

'She's eighty-six, quite small, and she's got grey hair and glasses,' Evie told them.

'Nae problem, love.' One of them ruffled William's hair. 'Don't you worry, son, we'll find your granny,' and off they dashed through the cavernous echoing station arches, Evie and William trailing behind.

The train was full of grey haired old ladies wearing glasses. The porters stopped each one to ask if their name was Mrs Wilson. Evie's mum stepped off, last, just as Evie and William caught up with the porters. Her grey hair was hidden under a red hat, and she didn't have her glasses on. She looked more like sixty than her eighty-six years.

Lots of everyday tasks can be equally tricky. Shopping in confined spaces is difficult, managing a wheelchair and a shopping trolley in a small supermarket involves superhuman skill – we always manage to get the one with the deviant left front wheel that defies steering. We tend to leave William to push himself around, but when we converge at the checkout he has invariably collected various items that have to be returned. 'No, the label says jelly, not Jedi, William. It has nothing to do with Star Wars!'

Trying on clothes in shops is impossible. If you need to pop out for a pint of milk, William has to be togged up, transferred into his wheelchair, taken out to the car, lifted into his car seat ('Don't worry William, honey, the sunroof isn't going to hurt you...'), his wheelchair has to be lifted into the back and the process reversed at the other end and repeated when you've got your pint of milk and again when you get home. I think we've become more organised since William arrived, but life can be hectic.

10

What lies ahead?

Evie's had one or two health scares over the last couple of years. She was rushed to hospital with abdominal pain, which turned out to be an ovarian cyst the size of a melon, and she spent a couple of weeks recovering from surgery. The year after that she had pneumonia and was on oxygen for ten days. Then she had symptoms of bowel cancer, but it turned out to be wind or some such. I'm a bit neurotic, but generally healthy. We each have iffy backs and are both well into our fifties. Our greatest fear is what would become of William if we both popped our clogs prematurely. When we were younger, two lots of friends bequeathed us their children if they, the parents, should die. We never got round to a formal arrangement for our older three, but Evie and I assumed that we'd have a bit of warning, and that probably my sister and Evie's brother and sister would step into our shoes if need be. But it's different for William. It's hard to find anyone who is comfortable about looking after him for a couple of hours, let alone for the rest of his life.

When I asked Ed for his thoughts about the adoption experience he wrote in his note:

Because of his cerebral palsy I do look at William and

115

worry what's going to happen when you two can't manage him anymore. Not meaning to sound selfish, but I sometimes worry that I'm going to have to come and take over the care of him, and as much as I love him I don't really feel I could do that. There are so many things that I want to do with my life that I wouldn't be able to if I had to look after William. That said, I would also feel bad if he was in a home or something, so I'm basically not wanting to have responsibility for all that.

Evie and I had no idea that Ed felt he might have to look after William one day. Needless to say, we got right on the phone and reassured him that there was absolutely no way he would end up caring for William, and that there were lots of specialist housing providers and domiciliary care projects that would put a package together when the time came, and help him to live as independently as possible. Sounds simple, doesn't it? We also assured him that we had no plans to die.

The nightmare scenario would be if we both died while William was still a child. As we said to Ed, we have no such plans, and you can't live your life based on "what ifs", can you? There's always risk and chance, but there's also hope and faith! The most likely future is a gentle decline of our physical abilities. As we become more decrepit, so the physical demands of caring for William will increase. He's getting heavier, and although he's becoming a little bit more independent, he still needs help with everything, unless he's watching TV or playing on the computer – although our computer seems to crash every ten minutes or so when William is on it, usually at a vital point in the cooking of the evening meal.

Over the years there has been a shift in the balance of demands posed by William. At first, the emotional demands were the most challenging for us as parents, and probably for the other children too. Although he still has spectacular outbursts, during which he comes out with the "I hate you and I never wanted to be part of this family" routine, these are easier to mange now because we know they will burn themselves out if we keep calm and stay consistent. And they are definitely lessening. But now the physical challenges are the greatest, particularly because the older three are less and less around to help.

Emotional demands are also still there, but they have changed in nature: whilst those relating directly to adoption have eased, those associated with social isolation have increased, and there are no practical solutions. We can install a ramp so that William can get in and out of the house more easily, but it is more difficult to install a friendship.

Our hope for William is that he will become more physically competent as we decline, so that by the time Evie and I are shuffling around on our Zimmer frames, he'll be able to transfer from his wheelchair on his own, and have a reasonable level of independence. On the positive side, Evie and I will both be retired by the time William is in his late teens. A constant problem we have at the moment is that it takes ages to do things right. It's so much quicker to lift William than to help him transfer from the wheelchair to the toilet seat. But when we retire, we'll have time to do it all properly. At least that's what we think now.

When he's in one of his loving moods, William tells us that he's never going to leave home. Who knows? There's some sheltered housing down the road from where we live, and maybe he'll choose to go somewhere like that, but it feels too early to plan that far ahead or even to think about it. We hope we'll have him established in some semi-independent set up when he's a young adult, so that he gets used to caring for himself with support before he's forced to by our creeping limitations. One concrete thing we have done is to make a will, with trustees, including our other three children and their aunts and uncles, to look after William's interests if the need should arise.

A more immediate and tangible concern is how William will manage the transitions to adolescence, secondary school, college and employment. And how will he cope with being the only child, when Robbie leaves home. The other night we left Robbie to boy-sit while we went out for a while, leaving strict instructions that William was to be in bed by eight thirty. When we got back at ten thirty, the two of them were furtively snacking on cheese and chocolate. William had told Robbie how much he missed Ed and Kate, prompting Robbie to indulge him with some brotherly attention. Who'll fill that gap when Robbie is away?

Friends who have children with disabilities have warned us that the secondary school years will be difficult. The two we know best have each transferred their children to special schools, at least on a part-time basis, because of concerns they were becoming socially isolated. The trouble is that we can't force children to befriend William out of a sense of duty; friendship has to come from real affection. It's hard to engineer friendships for him, but we'll keep trying.

There are college courses for young disabled school leavers, but some of them have the feel of time-filling about them rather than anything more constructive. There are one or two Trusts that are trying to develop more dignified and purposeful training programmes for disabled young people, and although it's still very early days, we have begun researching options, and have an increasingly fat file of information we are collecting along the way. At this stage, our job is to help William achieve his potential, without getting hung up about the fact that his academic progress is much slower than that of his peers. He may or may not pass any standard grades. What is important is that he feels good about who he is and has a sense of being fulfilled and happy.

Somewhere along the line, he could have a girlfriend (or a boyfriend). We sometimes find him exploring his body, like other children do, for pleasure and comfort, and are encouraging him to do it only in private. There are a lot of uncertainties ahead in terms of relationships he might or might not form and how these will impact on him, or how he'll cope with loneliness. We are trying to develop a network of supports to help him through life. He has wonderful godparents, who we are sure will be there for him in the years ahead. Ed, Kate and Robbie will be there too: not as carers but as siblings who love him.

Another challenge that lies somewhere in the future is the possibility of contact with his birth family. We just don't know if William will have the maturity to make a rational decision about whether to look them up when he is eighteen and has the legal right. We know of an adoption counselling service that will be able to help him. It wouldn't surprise us at all if he decides to make contact. He's very open and direct and I can imagine him saying straight out to his birth mother: 'Why did you not care for me and yet you cared for the others?' and I can see him getting the response that he was adopted against her wishes. It could be a messy business, and of course he'll need a lot of physical help as well as emotional support if he chooses to pursue contact. I know of adopted children who have gone back to their birth families at eighteen and rejected their adoptive families entirely. But William won't be able to just walk out; his options are limited. If we're not careful we could wander deeper and deeper into fantasy land!

Parenthood is a bit of a mystery journey, whether through birth or adoption. You can't know the final destination or the route or whether it will be smooth or bumpy. You just have to keep looking at the map and making decisions and enjoy the experience of travel and the here and now. When we set out on the adoption journey, we were as prepared as we could be. We were probably better prepared than many birth parents – we had experience of caring for children and we had lots of information about William, whereas all that most birth parents have is a fuzzy photo of a scan and maybe the result of an amniocentesis test. So far the journey has been a bit rockier than we had anticipated; it has taken us to places we would never otherwise have visited, but it has undoubtedly enriched us all. We've still got a long way to go, and we'll try to carry on travelling hopefully! As that wise old matriarch, Peggy Woolly of Ambridge, told her daughter Jennifer the other day, 'All you can do is to do your best and take one day at a time. That's all anyone can do.' What would we do without *The Archers?*

11

Would we do it again?

It's Sunday: I'm just finishing a mug of tea in bed. As usual, Evie has let the cup of peppermint infusion that I brought her get cold. 'I like it like that,' she always says, in a sleepy voice, when I complain to her about my wasted efforts. William needs to be got to his sports club for 10 am, so after I drain my mug and put down the novel I'm reading (it takes me weeks to plough through a novel these days) I haul myself out of bed, have a quick shower and go downstairs to make sure he's awake. I'm feeling a bit rough, and it's not as a result of too much vino collapso. Robbie went out last night and agreed he would be back at about midnight. He eventually came in at ten to three. Neither Evie nor I had slept, of course. Then I had to get up and make sure he was okay, check that he'd locked the door and switched everything off, and do a bit of nagging.

'Don't you realise how worried your mother and I have been?' I preached at him from the third stair. 'You said twelve at the latest.' I paused for effect, while poor Robbie shuffled about. 'And you've got to get to your Tesco job in the morning.'

'Yes, I know, I'm sorry.' At least he seemed to be

reasonably sober and unharmed. Parenthood, "The Family Business", is a mixed blessing.

I gently open William's door. His little ginger head raises itself above the piles of soft toys and second-hand naked action men figures he's bought from car boot sales. His movement triggers Buzz Lightyear to pipe up, 'I come in peace,' and we both giggle.

'Happy Father's Day,' says William cheerily, though I think he only just woke up as I opened the door.

I'd forgotten it was Father's Day. Not of course that I believe in that nonsense anyway – a festival imported from America to generate another commercial niche. Even so, I'd sent a card to my dad, and there's an irrational bit of me that wants it to be acknowledged by the kids.

'Oh, thank you, William,' I say and I bend down to give him a kiss on the cheek.

'You're the best daddy in the world,' he says, squirming among the toys. 'There's something under the bed for you.' I reach down and find two painted plant pots that Evie is obviously recycling from a box of unwanted gifts, but it's the thought that counts. There's also a handmade card, which William has painstakingly signed.

'What a beautiful card, and how did you know that I needed some posh flower pots, just like these?'

William smiles and I help him to urinate into his bottle. Then I dress his lower half, put on his splints and place his wheelchair beside the bed. While I'm busy he goes off on one of his rambles. He's preoccupied with the *Doctor Who* episode of the night before.

'Do you know Jack, Daddy, who the Daleks killed and who Rose brought back to life?' He thrashes about in his excitement. Buzz chips in: 'I am Buzz Lightyear.'

'Yes, we know who you are, don't we Will?'

William giggles.

Buzz continues: 'To infinity, and beyond!'

'Not till after breakfast, though, eh Will?'

'But Dad, Jack was in last night's episode. And do you know, he's now indestructible; he can't die anymore.'

'That's amazing.'

'Do you know, Dad, there have been ten Doctor Whos. They get a different actor every time he regenerates. The first one was William Hartnell, then there was Patrick Troughton, then Tom Baker...'

I put William's banana board handy – a curved yellow device which he uses to slide himself from the bed to the wheelchair – and give him the controller so that he can adjust the height of the electrically powered bed. Then I leave him to transfer, and to give me a shout if he gets stuck, while I cook the bacon and eggs. I keep to-ing and fro-ing between bedroom and kitchen to check that he's alright.

Eventually, after much calling of: 'Breakfast's on the table, Will...it's getting cold...come on, get a move on Will,' he trundles slowly through, singing, his face screwed up with the concentration. While we eat our bacon and egg, I notice the fine crop of daisies on the lawn; the grass is still too long, but it will never be manicured. If it dries out I might find time to cut it later. In the grand order of things it's not life's top priority. The rain has flattened the broad beans, and they spill untidily from one of the little vegetable patches I have cut into the lawn.

'Can I have a tape of *Doctor Who* on, Daddy?' William asks.

'Well, I'm quite enjoying this piano music, William, and it *is* Father's Day.'

'Yes, but you can listen to that when Mum and I have gone to sports club.'

'Okay. If you try and eat your breakfast by yourself.' We strike a deal, but he keeps forgetting to eat; multi-tasking is still too much for him. 'You know, William, I think your drooling is a little better; those tongue exercises that we got from Brainwave must be helping. You need to keep practising,' I say. He tries to push his cheek out from

123

the inside using his tongue – it's one of the prescribed exercises. The grass will always grow, but maybe William will stop drooling! A few moments later and he is miles away, engrossed in the story of Doctor Who. I shove a fork-full of bacon and egg into his mouth.

Evie comes in eating a piece of burnt toast. She insists that, as with the peppermint tea, she likes it that way. I'm not so sure. 'We must remember to order the new Harry Potter book,' she says.

'Must we?' I pull a face. The prospect of reading aloud another six hundred pages of Hogwarts wizardry is a bit much to contemplate on a Sunday morning.

'He loves it.'

'Yes, I know, I'm only joking.' I try to look convincing.

Evie and William are, as usual, a bit late setting off for the sports club. I wheel him out to the car, while Evie tries to rouse Robbie from his slumbers so that he won't be late for work. William won't let me put him in the car though – it's one of those days when he is afraid of the sunroof, and will get hysterical if I push it. (Damn that helium balloon!) But Evie comes at last and starts the engine. As usual that reassures him, so I ease him into his special car seat, we get the wheelchair into the boot and off they go. William gives me a wave and blows me a kiss as they pull away.

Shortly afterwards Robbie comes down in a crumpled shirt, and thrusts a Father's Day card at me, along with a gift of a packet of biscuits and some Man-size tissues. 'It's from Ed and me,' he says. The quirky present is a joke. It's the thought that counts, I tell myself again. Ed is home for the weekend, but he's still in bed. I'm sure I didn't waste my life away like that at his age…Robbie grabs a bowl of cereal. He declines my offer to iron his crumpled shirt. Despite his gift, I have to give him a bit more nagging for my disrupted night. 'I'm really sorry,' he says, before dashing out to work.

'And put your bowl in the dishwasher,' I call after him, but it's too late.

* * *

It's about six months since I started writing this book. It had to be put on hold when William was laid up with a severe chest infection for a month, and there was little time for anything much, but he's bounced back again. Now that he's gone off to sports club with Evie, I've got a bit of time to work on this, nearly the final chapter, though the story goes on of course – there is no final chapter in "The Family Business".

What would a birth parent say if asked, 'If you knew then what you know now, would you have children?' Most parents have some ambivalence about parenthood. It probably starts from the first pre-birth morning sickness, goes on through the pain of labour, the anxious early days and the sleepless nights. Then the disorder spreads into lives and homes that have been ordered, tidy and admired. The lifestyle changes: from exotic holidays and nights out to budget holidays with the car bulging with nappies, travel cots, bikes strapped to the back and complaining children. Games of rounders on the beach become compulsory, when all you really want to do is go off on your own or have a quiet drink in a country pub with only adults for company.

There's the endless anxiety too: little Johnny doesn't seem to have enough friends; he's not doing as well as he should at school. Your children have to have a full extracurricular programme, with piano lessons, cubs, football practice and family outings. And there are the teenage years: the sullen moodiness, the exams they won't study for, the people they are mixing with, the fear that they could be experimenting with drugs, the prospect of sex too young, the first vomit after excessive alcohol at two in the morning, when you have to be up at six the next day to get to an important meeting. And then they can end up despising you and leave home with hardly a backward glance.

It must be the "it'll never happen to me" syndrome that

keeps the human race having children. But of course it does happen again, and again. We've been unbelievably lucky, although we've had some of all the above. It would be a lie to say that we've enjoyed every minute of being parents, but on the whole it's been good, and we're proud of all four of our children; all very different in some ways, very alike in others, though they would never agree with that. So the question, "would we adopt again, if we knew then what we know now", is really irrelevant; it's a non-question. Would we have Ed, Kate and Robbie again? Of course.

We sometimes wonder what would have become of William if we had not adopted him. As far as we know we were the only family who expressed an interest in him, though he'd been publicised across the UK. Perhaps he'd have remained in foster care, though he'd probably have had to move to other carers; the family he was with had been saying for some time that they didn't feel able to care for him on a long-term basis. Maybe he'd have got lucky and ended up with another family; maybe he'd have needed residential care. Who knows? All of our family are clear that he's one of us; if you ask any of the other children whether adopting William was a good idea, they look at you as if there's a piece of your brain missing!

The one member of the family who is verbally the most ambivalent about the whole adoption business is William himself. In the morning he can say, 'I love you Daddy. You're the best daddy in the world. Give me a hug.' And you get all misty eyed and reach out to him. Then in the afternoon it can be, 'I don't want to come off the computer; I don't care if tea is ready; I never wanted to be in this family anyway; I'm leaving and I'm never coming back. I hate you...' The adopted child always has that other shadowy, secret world that can hurt them and that they can use to hurt you.

But for the whole family the question "would we do it again" is no more relevant in relation to William than it is in relation to the others. And the answer is a resounding "yes". That goes for our parents too. Evie's mum tagged along to a co-ordination meeting for William recently and gave her views about what she thought William needed. It was plain she was taking on the irrational advocate/grandparent role! My mum is quite frail now, but during a recent car journey I asked her what she really thought of us having adopted William. 'Oh, we all love William,' she said. 'Do you know I still say my prayers every night, and I always say a special one for William.' It's opened up new joys for our parents, and we're grateful to them for their support and value their commitment to William. We've even contemplated adopting again, or maybe fostering. William's godmothers nearly had collective apoplexy when we mentioned it. And of course they are right; it is a silly idea, but only because the adoption of another child would be hard for William to manage. We couldn't throw his life into disarray just when it seems to be settling down.

So, yes, we'd do it again, but would we have done things *differently* if we'd had the benefit of hindsight? Evie and I make mistakes every day in the way we parent William. For example, we know he needs consistency and we're sometimes not consistent. He is meant to go to bed at 8.30, but it's sometimes just too hard to pull yourself off the sofa to do the business, so it gets to be later. Then the next night William complains when we try to get him to bed at 8.30! We know he needs daily physio and exercises and sometimes we don't manage to fit them in. We know if he calls Robbie "Big Ears" it will escalate if we get cross, but we still get cross. Then there are the big questions. Is contact with his former foster carer really helpful to him, and us, in the long term? Is the contact with his birth brothers worth the distress he feels when they part? Were we right to put him through surgery to try and prevent his hamstrings tightening? Should we have kept him in specialist education – would he have been less isolated socially if we had?

William didn't come with an instruction manual. There was lots of information about his background and the nature of his disability, and there were lists of the routines he was used to, the things he would eat, and his bedtime rituals. We've had to put our own unwritten manual together about how to fully care for him as we've gone along, and as we have got to know William and grown to love and understand him. No doubt when he becomes a teenager we'll understand him less! We're still compiling the manual; still learning about what makes him tick and what works. We'll keep trying our best and I know we'll make lots more mistakes.

William has enriched us and our other children. Writing this book has led us to revisit our lives with William. We re-read his early life history the other day: his premature birth and subsequent withdrawal from opiates as a result of his birth mother's drug addiction; periods alone in hospital; nine different care arrangements in the first six months of his life; that sad little profile in the adoption magazine; the overwhelming grief he went through when he came to live with us and had to leave his foster carers; the struggle to find his sense of self in the light of being unwanted by his birth family; coming to terms with being a wheelchair user. And if that wasn't enough, it was then discovered that he had a visual impairment, he developed migraines and he was shunned by other children when he desperately wanted their friendship. Given all this, it is remarkable that he's as cheerful, loving and courageous as he is, and that he shows no shred of self-pity. He can light up a room with his infectious love of life. William is the hero of our "Family Business", and it is a privilege and a joy to be his parents.

12

Epilogue: tips and wrinkles

When Evie and I got married, one of our friends gave us a spoof wedding present of a little paperback book called *Tips and Wrinkles*. It has a subtitle: *A treasury of ways to save time and money around the home.* It contains all sorts of indispensable advice such as: 'To "iron" a handkerchief in an emergency, ease it out flat while still wet on a mirror or on the glass of a picture and leave until dry.' We've yet to encounter an emergency requiring an ironed hankie. We gave up ironing hankies years ago. The book quotes the definition of a "wrinkle" as 'a piece of information not generally known'.

This chapter contains tips and wrinkles about the adoption of children with disabilities. However, each adoption journey is different, just as each child is different. All advice and information therefore needs to be taken with a large pinch of salt, but here goes!

When I trained as a social worker in the dim and distant past, nearly all children "put up" for adoption were healthy babies. Older children and children with disabilities were generally brought up by foster carers or in care homes or institutions. Things have changed a lot. There are relatively few babies "available" for adoption these days; lone parents are supported to care for their children, contraception is freely available, and illegitimacy is no longer a disgrace. Nowadays, the children who need adoptive families are older; they may have suffered neglect or abuse or they may be disabled. They may have had a number of periods in care, and might find it difficult to form attachments. They can have behavioural or emotional problems that may last for years.

At the same time, there is no longer a stereotypical adoptive family. Adopters might be childless or they might have other children. They might be married, living with a partner, divorced, single, in same sex relationships, disabled, and from any racial, ethnic or religious background. And applicants don't need to be in the first flush of youth. The assessment of potential adopters now involves training, usually in a group setting, and a home study, which will focus particularly on gathering evidence to show that the applicants will make good enough parents. There are lots of children waiting for adoption and they don't need perfect parents!

You can't adopt on top of everything else you do – something will have to go. Children with disabilities take a lot of care and time. Try drawing a circle and dividing it into segments – each segment representing the amount of time you spend on the different things you do: stamp collecting, windsurfing, clay pigeon shooting, watching soaps or whatever. What are you prepared to give up in order to insert a large new childcare segment?

Our experience of being assessed and trained as adoptive parents was positive. It is important not to feel that you are being judged, but to use the process as an opportunity to learn, and a chance to work out whether adoption is for you. We know a number of people who have gone through the process and who have finally decided against adoption, but who have still found the experience personally valuable.

Once you reach the stage of being "matched" with a child, it is important to get as much information as you can before making a final commitment to proceed. However, William in the flesh was not the same as William in the pictures, or in the reports we'd read, and living with William was different again. Diagnoses and prognoses are useful up to a point, but labels are not, and it is important to have an open mind. We had thought William would eventually be able to walk using a frame, and then had to get used to the idea that this was not going to happen.

Adoptive parents get to know children in a way that others have not been able to. This might be stating the obvious: of course parents should know their children best! But it can lead to surprises and shocks. I know adoptive parents who have found out from their children that they have been sexually abused in the past, something that had not been known beforehand. It may be that children only feel able to make such disclosures from within the security of a "forever" family.

The first few months or years of caring for an adopted child can be particularly challenging. At the point of placement the child will be experiencing change and loss. They might be "testing" their new parents; the family might not be quite what they were expecting; they will have mixed feelings. Try putting yourself in their shoes for a while. Adoption is not often a soft-focused Anne of Green Gables story, either for the child or the adopters. But ultimately, most adoptions are successful in the grossly generalised meaning of the word.

Don't expect too much of yourself as an adoptive parent! You will probably feel that you aren't doing enough to help the child realise his or her full potential, or that despite all your best efforts, the child doesn't give much back, doesn't appreciate you and says cruel things to you. You can only do what you can do. It can be difficult to notice progress on a day-to-day basis; try to have six monthly reviews, whether formally with those involved in the child's care, health and education, or informally with friends and family, so you can acknowledge and mark progress.

Adopted children have birth families out there somewhere. There may be direct contact with them, indirect contact (through the exchange of photographs or letters) or no contact. Even if there is no contact, the birth family is part of the child's identity, and adoptive parents need to be able to feel comfortable in handling questions from the child about their other family. Contact, or even talking about the birth family, can trigger all sorts of mixed feelings in the child, and the fallout, distress and anger can last for days. It is generally healthier to allow the child to express these real feelings than to suppress them. Adopted children can build up rosy fantasies about their birth families. If there is direct contact, the child, the adopters and the birth family should be offered professional support.

Much of the support Evie and I get for managing "the Family Business" comes from each other. It is essential to talk to your partner about how you feel, and about all the little problems that will arise each day. If you haven't got a partner, choose a special friend.

As a parent you can expect to lose your temper and to be grumpy and nag, but try and de-brief yourself afterwards, and talk it over with the child. If criticism of children who have been brought up in a *secure* environment from birth is to be effective, it needs to be balanced with praise. As a rule of thumb, one critical comment needs to be offset by three positive ones. So, 'Charlie, you've left your shoes in the middle of the floor *again*,' only has a chance of making an impression if you balance it with, say,

'Thanks, Charlie, for clearing your plate away – that's really helpful,' *and* 'you got on with your homework really quickly today,' *and* 'I really enjoyed going shopping with you today, Charlie!' Adopted children need at least *six* statements of praise for each criticism. Some say they need as many as twenty! Incessant nagging doesn't work, but it's easier said than done.

In our admittedly very limited experience, children with disabilities have all the same emotional problems as other adopted children, including loss, disrupted attachment and poor self-esteem. These can be just as hard to deal with as the disability itself.

We have found that William glows with pleasure if he can get a sense of achievement from doing something. For example, he can swim a little, ride his trike and work the computer. It's important to keep trying to find new, stimulating activities for children with limited abilities. We recently entombed some new mysterious toy knights in a block of plaster of Paris and William excavated them using my hammer. It took him two days to complete the job and afterwards there was plaster ground into all his clothes, but it gave him a real sense of satisfaction, and helped his co-ordination and concentration skills.

If you have more than one child, make sure you give each one some individual time. This might seem fairly obvious, but it is easy to get into a routine revolving around the family group and the disabled child, and everyone needs some one-to-one time, though my older children suddenly seem to have something urgent to do when I suggest a walk or try to recruit one of them to help me to cook the dinner.

If you're not naturally assertive, go to classes! You need to be able to speak up for your child, sometimes in intimidating settings. Rehearse what you want to say before you go to the meeting. We have also found it very helpful to have an ally in some meetings. The worker at our local

Princess Royal Trust Carers' Centre has been particularly good at advocating our needs and William's needs at various review meetings. Her experience, knowledge and dispassionate objectivity shine through.

Unless you are one of those serene, unflappable types, take up yoga as an aid to maintaining your cool. If you haven't time for yoga, counting to ten, slowly, is a fair substitute when you're feeling stressed.

Adopting a child with disabilities is hard work. Take all the financial, practical and emotional help you are offered and then ask for more! It took us ages to find out about financial help and benefits that can be available. It's way beyond the scope of this book to give a comprehensive directory of relevant legislation and sources of help and support, but some of the following clues might point you in the right direction. Access to a computer with internet and a search engine is just about essential. Do as much research as possible *before* the child arrives.

Legislation about adoption is changing and is different in Scotland, England and Wales and Northern Ireland. Make sure you are clear about the legal status of the child and the court procedures that might lie ahead. Check how the costs of any legal processes will be met. There should be a post-placement adoption plan for the child, setting down what support you can expect from the local authority that "looked after" the child. Once the adoption has been finalised, the local authority where you live (which might be different from the one that placed the child) should not discriminate against you or the child because the child is adopted. Try and get the placing local authority to be clear about which authority is responsible for what from the outset.

If you adopt a child with additional needs, he or she might attract an *adoption allowance*. This is payable by the local authority which had legal responsibility for the child prior to placement, and payments can continue for as long as the child remains in full-time education. The criteria for an allowance are complex, but roughly speaking require that the child will incur care costs which will be greater than for other children, and that adoption would not be practicable without the payment of an allowance. Applicants are means tested, and adoption allowance schemes can vary between local authorities, so that a child might attract an allowance in one part of the country, but not in another.

There are a number of national and local organisations that provide advice and support to adopters. Support can include counselling, training and mutual support groups for adopters and their children. You should be able to find details on the internet. Some of the organisations are run by adopters.

Local authorities have a number of duties and powers in relation to children with disabilities. Again, some of the legislation in Scotland is different from that in England and Wales and Northern Ireland. As a common principle, local authorities have statutory duties to assess the needs of disabled people for support and services. Disabled people should be entitled to an assessment of their needs in respect of:

- practical assistance in the home, such as domiciliary care;
- assistance in taking advantage of educational facilities;
- transport to and from home in relation to certain services;
- aids and adaptations – we have had help with the costs of installing a downstairs shower room and have been offered help with a ramp up to the front door;
- assistance with holidays;
- dietary requirements;
- assistance in obtaining a telephone. A social worker, occupational therapist or care manager from the social services or social work department usually carries out

assessments. Sometimes there can be quite a wait to get an assessment.

Local authorities have finite budgets and are not always able to provide what has been assessed as needed. There are complaints and appeals procedures if you are dissatisfied with the service, or lack of it.

Children affected by disability may be subject to a number of other statutory assessments, and local authorities should try to complete these concurrently or combine them. These assessments can be difficult for parents to respond to, not only because of the inherent labelling of the child, but also because of the seeming judgements that are made by people who have minimal contact with your child.

People with disabilities (or their carers) can apply for *direct payments*, now sometimes called "self-directed support" (just when you get used to one form of terminology, they change it), to employ carers or pay for care agencies privately. The idea behind this is to empower people with disabilities and their carers to make their own arrangements, in ways that can be closely tailored to their needs. We have enquired about direct payments in relation to William a number of times, but have been advised that there are no funds available.

The law relating to the education of children with disabilities varies depending on which part of the UK you live in. Education authorities in the UK now generally accept the principle of "inclusion". New laws mean schools, colleges and universities cannot treat disabled students "less favourably" than non-disabled students. And they must make "reasonable adjustments" to ensure disabled students are not disadvantaged compared to their non-disabled peers. These new laws cover school admissions, exclusions and education and associated services, including school trips and after-school clubs and activities.

Schools and local authorities must now also draw up strategic plans to make it easier for disabled pupils to be taught in mainstream schools. They must:

- improve physical access to buildings with ramps, handrails and lifts;
- make lessons more accessible through staff training and class organisation;
- make information more easily available through handouts and timetables in large print, Braille or audio tape.

There are still lots of specialist schools for children with disabilities. Parents, children and educationalists can have different views, often strongly held, about whether inclusion or specialism is better. The education authority/department will assess the child's needs, usually with the involvement of an educational psychologist. There are appeals procedures if parents and children disagree with the local authority about the provision that is offered. There are advocacy and mediation services to help and support parents with this process. Each child with additional needs should have a co-ordinated education support plan, or its equivalent, and this plan should be reviewed regularly.

There are a number of state benefits for children with disablities that are the same all over the UK. A *Disability Living Allowance* (DLA) might be payable if the disabled person has needed help for three months and is likely to need assistance for at least a further six months. There are two components to DLA. The Care Component can be claimed for a child of any age who requires special personal care or help with communicating. It can also be paid for deaf or visually impaired children or for a child who needs someone to be with them in order to stop them hurting themselves or other people. There are specfic criteria for children who are terminally ill. The Mobility Component can be claimed for a child over three who is unable to walk or has difficulty walking because of their disability, or for children over five if they can walk, but need someone with them to ensure they are safe or to help them find their way around. DLA is paid on behalf of the child and is not means tested.

Parents of adopted children are entitled to *child benefit*, the same as other parents.

A *Carer's Allowance* may be payable to adopters on a low income who look after a person over the age of sixteen with an illness or disability, who is not in full-time education.

Increased levels of *Child Tax Credit* are payable to people with children who have disabilities, depending on their income.

The Family Fund Trust is a government-funded charity which provides money to buy equipment or services for children with disabilities. Applicants are means tested. There are other charitable Trusts that give funds for specialist equipment, holidays and activities for disabled children. It is sometimes possible to access assistance even if you have a reasonably good income.

A *disabled parking badge* (Blue Badge) can be issued by the local authority. Children can be eligible if they have mobility problems or are registered blind. But don't forget to renew it as it is not given for life and there is no reminder!

People, including children, claiming the higher rate of the mobility component of DLA can be exempted from road tax, but the vehicle must be used only for the disabled person.

If your home has been adapted to meet the needs of a disabled person, you may be eligible for a reduction in council tax.

If your child is registered blind you may get a 50 per cent reduction in the cost of a TV licence.

In most parts of the country disabled children and their attendant can get free transport on local buses. There may be concessions on rail travel, certain ferries and toll bridges.

There is a national network of accessible public toilets, for which it is necessary to buy a key. Evie has a mini unpublicised campaign to use the term "accessible" in relation to toilets/parking spaces/buses, etc, because if they were "disabled" as they are often labelled, they might not work particularly well! You can get a bit touchy when you're in the disability world.

Many local and national organisations provide services to families with disabled children. Contact a Family is a national charity which offers support and advice to parents whose children have special needs or disabilities, regardless of their particular medical condition. Their website has a directory of specific conditions and rare syndromes and they specialise in putting families in touch with each other.

The disability world has a dizzying aray of professionals with whom you may be in contact at some stage. Here are a few of the main ones and a summary of their roles.

Occupational therapists (OTs) are trained to look at how to maximise self-help. They can provide appropriate equipment and adaptations to the home and can advise and help people with disabilities to adapt to their environment. OTs can be based in health departments or local authorities and work in a variety of settings: child development centres, nurseries, schools (mainstream and special schools), at home or in hospitals. Examples of the help we have had from OTs include adaptations to the home and aids to daily living, such as special cutlery that is easy to hold, toilet seating, devices to help transfer from wheelchair to bed and so on.

Paediatric Physiotherapists are concerned with the assessment, treatment and management of children who have a general developmental delay, mobility disorder, disability or illness which may be improved, controlled or alleviated by physiotherapy and/or the use of specialised equipment. In our experience, the physiotherapy service can be very stretched, and the amount of direct contact may therefore be limited. Physiotherapists can be helpful in devising exercise programmes to counter the effects of progressive conditions and to develop mobility skills. They can provide equipment, such as walking frames, to aid mobility.

The *Speech and Language Therapy Service* aims to promote the child's communication and/or eating and drinking skills. Therapists can offer advice and assistance in relation to problems of swallowing and drooling. Children can access this therapy from birth, for example, if a child is born with a cleft palate, or has eating/drinking difficulties, or Down's syndrome.

Community and hospital-based *Audiometricians* work with paediatricians in assessing hearing impairment.

The *Community Paediatric Service* undertakes medical assessments of children with developmental, behavioural or learning difficulties that may have an underlying medical cause. Community paediatricians provide advice and support to parents, young people, teachers and a wide range of professionals working in other agencies.

The range and number of therapists and others will vary depending on the nature your child's disability. It is worth trying to build good relations with them (we are all human) and choosing one or two who can act as "key workers" and who might help to co-ordinate services.

If you become the parent of a disabled child, you will come across physical barriers, social injustices and obstacles to the inclusion of your child in all sorts of ways. You are likely to get cross and frustrated and to want to change things. There are both national and local campaign groups, and you may find that the statutory agencies are sometimes hungry for your views about how services should be developed. You may even be asked to join a focus group.

Change happens slowly, and the process is frustrating, with similar questions being asked over and over, and findings and reports being set out in glossy booklets that often state the obvious but don't seem to lead anywhere. But things are improving. When you enter the Family Business and the disability world, it is essential to stay upbeat, to speak up for your child and to retain your sense of humour. As the Monty Python song goes: 'Always look on the bright side of life!'

The other day, while we were eating our tea, the subject of "how lucky we are" came up in conversation. I can't remember what triggered it; I think there had been a report on the news about a natural disaster in a far-off place, with images of misery, grief and poverty.

'Yes, we're so lucky to live where we do and have everything we need,' said Evie.

'So try and finish the last couple of mouthfuls of dinner, William,' I said. 'Think of those poor children who don't have enough to eat.' I knew immediately that was a silly thing to say, and of course William retorted:

'Why don't we send it to them, then? Anyway, it tastes a bit burnt to me,' he added mischievously, glancing at Evie.

I pushed a forkful of pasta between his lips, which parted as it approached, like a baby sparrow's beak, and he chomped away for a few moments. Then he said, 'I think I am really lucky.'

'That's good, William,' said Evie. 'Why do you think that?'

He scooped up the remains of his dinner, put it into his mouth by himself, and began chewing; taking his time; keeping us in suspense.

Would he tell us that he was lucky because he had nice parents, maybe? Or because he had such lovely brothers and a sister? Or because he was part of a happy family?

The answer, when it came at last, didn't feature any of these things. 'I'm lucky because I'm so cool,' he said.

Having finished tea, William trundled into the living room. He's just discovered the doubtful delights of *YouTube* and wanted to look at the latest McFly video and join in with the singing. He paused for a quick look at himself in the hall mirror on the way.

Afterwards, when we thought about it, Evie and I agreed that it was the best answer William could have given. Despite all he has to put up with in life, he feels he's "cool". He has a sense of feeling good about himself and secure about his place in the world. What more could parents wish for?